WRITING COMPELLING DIALOGUE FOR FILM AND TV

Writing Compelling Dialogue for Film and TV is a practical guide that provides you, the screenwriter, with a clear set of exercises, tools, and methods to raise your ability to hear and discern conversation at a more complex level, in turn allowing you to create better, more nuanced, complex, and compelling dialogue.

The process of understanding dialogue writing begins with increasing writers' awareness of what they hear. This book provides writers with an assortment of dialogue and language tools, techniques, and exercises, and teaches them how to perceive and understand the function, intent, and thematic/psychological elements that dialogue can convey about character, tone, and story. Text, subtext, voice, conflict, exposition, rhythm, and style are among the many aspects covered. This book reminds us of the sheer joy of great dialogue and will change and enhance the way writers hear, listen to, and write dialogue, and along the way aid the writers' confidence in their own voice allowing them to become more proficient writers of dialogue.

Written by veteran screenwriter, playwright, and screenwriting professor Loren-Paul Caplin, *Writing Compelling Dialogue* is an invaluable writing tool for any aspiring screenwriter who wants to improve their ability to write dialogue for film and television, as well as students, professionals, and educators.

Loren-Paul Caplin has written feature films and TV scripts for studios and independents, including Paramount, Universal, Sony, and Fox Searchlight. He teaches and has taught screenwriting at Columbia University, NYU/Tisch Department of Dramatic Writing, The New School (where he coauthored the Screenwriting Certificate Curriculum), and Hofstra University. He also wrote/ directed the feature *The Lucky Ones* (Tribeca Film Festival, 2003) and short film *The History of the World in 8 Minutes* (New Directors/New Films Festival, MoMA) as well as several plays, and has done commentary for Criterion Collection and is a screenwriting consultant.

WRITING COMPELLING DIALOGUE FOR FILM AND TV

The Art & Craft of Raising Your Voice on Screen

Loren-Paul Caplin

Routledge
Taylor & Francis Group

LONDON AND NEW YORK

First published 2021
by Routledge
2 Park Square, Milton Park, Abingdon, Oxon OX14 4RN

and by Routledge
52 Vanderbilt Avenue, New York, NY 10017

Routledge is an imprint of the Taylor & Francis Group, an informa business

© 2021 Loren-Paul Caplin

British Library Cataloguing-in-Publication Data
A catalogue record for this book is available from the British Library

Library of Congress Cataloging-in-Publication Data
A catalog record has been requested for this book

ISBN: 978-0-367-25687-6 (hbk)
ISBN: 978-0-367-25686-9 (pbk)
ISBN: 978-0-429-28915-6 (ebk)

Typeset in Bembo
by Deanta Global Publishing Services, Chennai, India

CONTENTS

ACKNOWLEDGMENTS

Robert Frost insightfully said, "I write to find out what I didn't know I knew." Although I have found this absolutely true in my life of dramatic writing, I was constantly surprised how true it was while writing this book.

I would like to thank Routledge, especially Sheni Kruger who first approached me about this project, and Sarah Pickles who continued to guide me through to the end.

While writing this book, my intern, Ellen Y. Xing, has been invaluable, both with line editing and as a sounding board. I am extremely grateful for her enthusiastic and skilled assistance.

I want to thank two students, Sydney Epstein from the New School, and Clio Yang from Barnard College, who allowed me to use a couple of excerpts of their excellent class assignments.

I would also like to take this opportunity to thank Annette Insdorf – film studies professor at Columbia University and mentor – who enabled me to begin the journey of teaching. Her generosity of spirit has been a constant inspiration.

I'd like to acknowledge my friends and family, especially Judith and Brian Forst and Ian Krieger, who continuously helped to keep me on point.

Finally, I would like to thank my wife, artist Jenne van Eeghen-Caplin, for her love and support and shared understanding of the creative process.

FADE IN: INTRODUCTION

Dialogue is the music of the written script. Everything else is what we see or imagine in our mind's eye. But when we get to the dialogue, we *hear* it.

* * *

For the longest time, I believed that you couldn't teach someone to write great dialogue. Like in music, how could you teach a guitar player to play as well as, say, Eric Clapton? With dialogue, we're all equivalent to "a guitar player." We all know how to speak, and if pressed, we could all write down some of that "speak" on paper. And, that would qualify as dialogue. But how do we turn that speech into Shakespeare? Or more to the point in film and TV, how can you turn that speech into something that is as hot as dialogue by Aaron Sorkin, Quentin Tarantino, Diablo Cody, Paddy Chayefsky, David Mamet, Nora Ephron, the Coen brothers, Vince Gilligan, Noah Hawley, Nic Pizzolatto, or Melissa Rosenberg ... to name but a few?

After decades of writing professionally and teaching screenwriting, what I have found is that it is possible. Not necessarily to turn a novice screenwriter into an equivalent Eric Clapton or any number of brilliant dialogue writers, but, *with devotion and hard work, it is possible to raise anyone's game higher than where they started.* And with the understanding that to be a working screenwriter one doesn't have to and/or doesn't need to write "brilliant" dialogue in order to be successful, suddenly the task of raising one's ability to a "workmanlike" level is more than enough ... and achievable. Workmanlike dialogue, however, is still a very high bar. It still needs to be serviceable, appropriate to the tone, and authentic, and this too takes devotion, training, *understanding,* and ability. I compiled a set of practical tools and exercises that can help accomplish that. And along with understanding, focus, some talent, empathy, and luck, who knows, one might even be able to write dialogue that sings like a great song.

For the most part, the actual words used in writing dialogue are the same for film and television (premium, streaming, etc.). However, the difference between the forms might require various adjustments – mostly story-wise. There is less time in a feature film than in a television series. Commercials might dictate certain story demands. Sitcoms are more specific to the small screen. And each of these differences might use dialogue toward implementing what is required. (More about this in Chapter Five.) But what is covered in this book is designed to inform both film and television dialogue writing equally.

* * *

It is a common notion among beginning screenwriters (and playwrights) that they believe their dialogue is better than others actually perceive it to be. Why is this? Inside their heads, the way that they hear their own words being spoken (possibly imagined by their favorite stars) with just the right inflections, specific background music playing, and with all their personal intentions and emotions built-in – it sounds perfect. But it's not that perfect when actually heard, or even read, by others. Maybe it's even far from perfect.

Scripted dialogue does not necessarily have to be "realistic." Most of the time it is not. That is why it is scripted. We only *aspire* to speak as eloquently or as comedic or as tough as our favorite characters do. But workable dialogue needs to be at least appropriate to the characters and tone of the narrative. It has to be believable within the world of your storytelling.

Often, when writers write dialogue, they seem to be channeling some mysterious place almost outside of themselves, even if it is simply inside their minds. A writer, for example, might transcribe exactly all of the lines that her various characters are saying in her mind's ear – and that alone can be an exhilarating experience. There's something uniquely special about "hearing" the voices of our characters. And simultaneously, capturing them on paper for eternity, verges between exquisite madness and what can feel like some kind of revelatory phenomena. Don't they say that if you pray to God, you're sane, but if you hear God answer back, you're insane? New writers are amazed at how clearly they might hear the dialogue in their heads and how fast pages of conversation mount up. It's understandable that this strange and alien experience is proudly coveted, even regarded as hyperauthentic (how do you doubt revelation?) and given great value. Plus, there are all the pages to prove that it actually happened. It wasn't a delusion.

Unfortunately, as real as the words on the pages are, and as effortlessly mystical and exciting that the experience of writing them feels, none of this automatically makes what was written great dialogue – or even good-enough dialogue. Great dialogue is rare, and the ability to write it comes from a combination of natural talent, awareness and skill, hard work, and great focus. We can't worry or compare ourselves to the rarified outlier who preternaturally and seamlessly writes brilliant dialogue without trying. This book is for those who are not naturally as eloquent as Shakespeare, or who don't possess the gifts of the hyperintelligent gab artists like Sorkin, or cannot easily access the incredibly compelling patois of Tarantino, but still want to have aspects of that caliber dialogue in their own dialogue writing. And that is possible.

When I started out as a young writer, my friends were marveled by how fast I could complete entire full-length plays, as if speed was a sign of excellence. Yes, the experience of finding that waterfall-flow of words and being ultrafocused and productive was, and still is, intoxicating. But I quickly learned that although I could literally channel an entire cocktail party, hear it in my mind, and seamlessly transcribe it, it wasn't a good enough channel; the dialogue from that cocktail party wasn't unique and interesting enough, didn't reveal the nuances of character enough, and wasn't as compelling or entertaining as I had believed, as I heard and transcribed it. It was painful that others didn't feel as enthusiastic as I felt while I was writing it. Was it a matter of changing channels or improving upon what I initially wrote down and realizing that it was the first draft? It's tough to change channels, since that has to do with your neural wiring, the hand you're dealt. But you can raise the level of dialogue that you do write.

* * *

Writing Compelling Dialogue for Film and TV: The Art & Craft of Raising Your Voice on Screen is designed to immerse writers, students, professional screenwriters, and instructors of dramatic writing (film, TV, theater, and aspects of prose) into the art and craft of writing dialogue. It is a practical guide to literally raising one's ability to write better, more unique, authentic (when appropriate), and compelling dialogue. Great dialogue grabs the attention of readers and attracts actors; it also pleases and thrills audiences. Strong dialogue can make the difference between a professional and unprofessional script, a salable script, let alone a successfully produced script.

Starting with an in-depth discussion and explanation of the meaning and intent of dialogue — its usage, context, and the thematic/psychological elements that dialogue can convey about character, tone, and story — the book will also include a description of the various dialogue types and their specific tones vis-à-vis their various platforms (film, TV, theater, and prose). The reader will then be given an extensive and unique set of practical tools and *exercises* to enhance their dialogue writing. Along the way, as well as with each "tool," there will be excerpted examples from produced and unproduced scripts. The specific exercises are designed to raise one's awareness of the myriad aspects of dialogue as well as enhance one's ability to literally raise the quality of one's dialogue writing. For those who don't have the time or patience to practice the exercises, there will also be examples of the exercises and their transitions into improved dialogue.

My compendium of devices or tools, or as I call it "tool kit," consists of a list of very specific aspects of language, grammar, and literary devices that, when incorporated and applied to most sentences of dialogue, has a potentially transformative effect. I've never seen a coherent list of practical tools such as this assembled in one place. My exercises are the result of not only my own dialogue-writing practices as a playwright, TV, and film writer, but also from years of working with students in dialogue and screenwriting classes. They are designed to, among other things, raise one's perception of hearing spoken words. I call it "ear tuning."

Readers will be given an assortment of dialogue/language tools while learning to perceive and understand the function, intent, and thematic/psychological elements that dialogue can convey about character, tone, and story. Text, subtext, intentions, goals and inner goals, voice, conflict, exposition, rhythm, and style are among the many aspects covered. Writers will enhance their access to their own voice while employing specific dialogue writing tools.

Invariably, when thinking about dialogue it is impossible to entirely compartmentalize one aspect from another. For example, one wouldn't ignore subtext when considering specific word choices. Or forget intent when considering rhythm. Consequently, there is some overlap and repeats throughout the various chapters.

There are plenty of basic "what not to do" rules. There just aren't as many "what to do" rules and more importantly "why." And, there aren't many go-to sources of how to automatically improve dialogue writing. Since for many writers, there is this nagging, chronic insecurity on the subject of dialogue writing, I began to wonder if superlative dialogue could be decoded in a similar way that screenwriting structure has been decoded for others to follow and imitate.

What I found is that it is possible. As I've said, this is not to automatically turn every screenwriter into an Aaron Sorkin or any number of brilliant dialogue writers, but instead, to raise anyone's game higher than where they started. At minimum, to appreciate in greater depth the dynamics of dialogue. Additionally, throughout this book, when I speak about dialogue and its ability to reveal depth of character, I often switch from referring to "your characters" and "you," i.e., your own subjective experience. In doing this, I'm hoping that when writers seek references, examples, and inspiration for great dialogue, including sources of motivation for great dialogue, that they not only search the incredible library of films that are available, but also examine their own lives and listen to their own voices.

Finally, *Writing Compelling Dialogue for Film and TV* wants to remind us of the purpose and joy of great dialogue while providing greater understanding, tools, techniques, and exercises to enhance our ability to pull it off.

PART ONE
On dialogue

Part One is devoted to expanding the entire subject of dialogue, dialogue writing, and its various forms within film and television. This includes introducing various terms and concepts that are commonly used when discussing dialogue writing. Beginning with the basics, dialogue's function and purpose is about gaining a deeper understanding of the numerous qualities that are innate to functional and viable scripted conversations. These qualities are among the more subtle aspects that current screen and television writers must constantly gauge. Tone, style, and subtext are among the concepts covered. There is also a thorough analysis of monologues, voice-overs, and other forms of characters' intoning on screen. Part One also explores the dynamics of *character* and how dialogue can inform the most complex aspects of personality. Fictional narrative writers are invariably tasked with the job of being psychologists as they lead their characters through their story's permutations in a cogent, even if bizarre, journey. In Chapter Two, "Illuminating Characters through Dialogue," the notion of dialogue as a key method for externalizing characters' inner lives is thoroughly discussed. The basics covered in Part One are the bedrock of understanding dialogue and what is required in writing dialogue successfully.

1

UNDERSTANDING DIALOGUE

Introduction: Understanding dialogue

Let's start at the beginning. Way before "In the beginning was the Word," there were biological entities that *reacted* to their environment. The purpose of this "reaction" was to aid in the survival of the entity. The biological entity *needed* specific resources and conditions in order for it to survive. To say that they *wanted* these basic resources is likely incorrect since there's little evidence that minimal-cell biological entities have *consciousness*, *agency*, or even *choice*. They are alive, *act* according to their genetic codes, and react to their environment in the service of surviving. But would it be too much of a stretch if we posited the idea that all biological entities are in *communication* with their environment? After all, there appears to be a back and forth reactivity; there certainly is an ongoing connection between the entity and its surroundings. Isn't this communication?

I'm hoping that you know where I'm going with all this talk of biology. In dramatic writing, and in the process of theatrical acting, the exact same notions are at the root of understanding and creating character: *wants*, *needs*, *choice*, *agency*, *consciousness*, *reactions*, *actions*, *survival*, and *communication*. These are among the terms and concepts that we think about regarding understanding and building characters. And it follows, what's on their minds – and what they might speak about: dialogue.

Function and purpose

In broad terms, the function and purpose of dialogue in film and television is to move the story along, illuminate character, and/or be entertaining. The domain of building story and plot lies within understanding the story-writing process. However, here we are focusing on understanding and writing the dialogue that helps that process.

When we think about dialogue, we think about communication. Usually this entails two or more poles or terminals: the sender and the receiver. Sending connotes information, data, emotion, interest, and even physical material. Even though a terminal can be both a sender and receiver, when we think of two poles interacting, they are usually sentient and conscious entities. But it doesn't always have to be two conscious entities, or even a two-way communication. Isn't it possible to communicate with nature, with a tree, the ocean, the sky, or a teddy bear? One can communicate and emotionally connect with an inanimate object or a less conscious entity, like an animal in a one-way flow by just sending. So it seems, that of the two poles, *the sender* appears to take precedent, has greater agency, and can even act independently. Animals and humans send and seek information by way of sounds, language, body language, body sensors, and gestures. And most of this information has to do with survival, wants, and needs. This brings us to humans and word language, as opposed to body language and gestures.

Dialogue comes from the Greek root *dia* ("through," "between," or "across") and *logue* ("discourse" or "speak"). The idea of speaking through, between, or across something parallels our basic biological entity communicating with and through its environment. This concept of communicating and being in communication with one's environment is at the heart of why we, as humans, talk. Dialogue, the way we're using the term in this book, is human communication expressly spoken in a scripted space. Spoken communication in its scripted version is dialogue. *Dialogue is how characters verbally engage with the world.*

Scripted dialogue includes monologues and voice-overs, but in film and TV, not unlike in life, when characters engage with the world outside of themselves, this means primarily engaging with other characters. I'm stressing here the importance of not being confined to film and TV examples when we think about scripted characters and how, what, and why they speak to each other. *In thinking about dialogue, its function and purpose, it's wise to think beyond the artifice of scripted material.* As we consider what makes great dialogue, we need to also consider what makes great talking among friends, intimate conversation between lovers, and all verbal communication outside of the scripted dramatic arena. There are indeed often differences, but the essence is the same: connection.

But let's examine some of the differences between real-life communication and scripted communication, dialogue.

When we talk about "great" communication or a great conversation in real life, it often means, among many things, being understood, acknowledged, entertained, learning, and entertaining. It often is pleasurable, exhilarating, energetic, and even provocative. We all know the feeling of engaging in a free-flowing, stimulating exchange. Add humor and wit and we find ourselves participating at a level of communication that even surprises ourselves. This is as though you are playing tennis with a much better player and in doing so, your own game rises to a higher skill set. In real life, the other side of "great" communication might be a horrible argument. We wouldn't call this great if we were participating in it. But we might if we were listening to it, if it wasn't us. So, great dialogue, as opposed to a real-life conversation, might not be about being understood as much as the frustration and struggle of attempting to be understood. Often, it is this struggle that makes great dialogue, but a disturbing reality.

Picture that you've come to your ex-spouse's place of work to inform him that you have gotten engaged. Uncomfortable, awkward. Who talks like this?

>   BURNS
>   (not noticing her yet)
>   What do you want?
>
>   HILDY.
>   Why, I'm surprised, Mr. Burns. That's
>   no way to talk to your wife -- even
>   if she's no longer your wife.
>
>   BURNS
>   (grinning)
>   Hello, Hildy!

A few moments later they get into it:

>   HILDY
>   May I have a cigarette, please?
>
>   HILDY
>   Thanks. A match?
>
>   BURNS
>   How long is it?
>
>   HILDY
>   How long is what?
>
>   BURNS
>   You know what. How long since we've
>   seen each other?

                    HILDY
Let's see. I was in Reno six weeks --
then Bermuda ... Oh, about four months,
I guess. Seems like yesterday to me.

                    BURNS
          (slyly)
Maybe it was yesterday. Been seeing
me in your dreams?

                    HILDY
          (casually)
No -- Mama doesn't dream about you
any more, Walter. You wouldn't know
the old girl now.

                    BURNS
          (with conviction)
Oh, yes I would. I'd know you any
time --

               BURNS AND HILDY
          (together)
-- any place, anywhere --

                    HILDY
          (half-pityingly)
You're repeating yourself! That's
the speech you made the night you
proposed.
          (she burlesques his
          fervor)
"-- any time -- any place --
anywhere!"

                    BURNS
          (growling)
I notice you still remember it.

                    HILDY
I'll always remember it. If I hadn't
remembered it, I wouldn't have
divorced you.

                    BURNS
You know, Hildy, I sort of wish you
hadn't done it.

                        HILDY
Done what?

                        BURNS
Divorced me. It sort of makes a fellow
lose faith in himself. It almost
gives him a feeling he wasn't wanted.

                        HILDY
Holy mackerel! Look, Walter, that's
what divorces are for.

                        BURNS
Nonsense. You've got the old-fashioned
idea that divorces are something
that last forever -- till 'death us
do part'. Why, a divorce doesn't
mean anything today. It's only a few
words mumbled over you by a judge.
We've got something between us nothing
can change.

                        HILDY
I suppose that's true in a way. I am
fond of you, Walter. I often wish
you weren't such a stinker.

                        BURNS
Now, that's a nice thing to say.

                        HILDY
Well, why did you promise me you
wouldn't fight the divorce and then
try and gum up the whole works?

                        BURNS
Well, I meant to let you go -- but,
you know, you never miss the water
till the well runs dry.

                        HILDY
A fellow your age, hiring an airplane
to write:
        (she gestures above
        to indicate sky-
        writing)
'Hildy: Don't be hasty -- remember
my dimple. Walter.!' It held things

```
up twenty minutes while the Judge
ran out to watch it.

                BURNS
Well, I don't want to brag, but I've
still got the dimple -- and in the
same place -- I just acted like any
husband who doesn't want to see his
home broken up.

                HILDY
What home?

                BURNS
What home? Don't you remember the
home I promised you?

                HILDY
Oh, yes -- we were to have it right
after our honeymoon -- honeymoon!
```

The answer to the question of who talks like this is Cary Grant and Rosalind Russell in the film *His Girl Friday* (dir. Howard Hawks, 1940). The movie is based on the play *Front Page* written by Ben Hecht and Charles MacArthur. Smart, sassy, and fast-talking, it's the way we wish we spoke if we wanted to emulate attractive, sophisticated white adults from a certain time period. It's entirely stylized and unreal and yet we follow the back-and-forth banter, the logic of their exchange, with rapt attention. Why? Because we know, or can imagine, the emotional awkwardness of any recently divorced couple forced to communicate, and enjoy how deftly and wittily they navigate those waters. We are suddenly a fly on the wall of a world that is likely far from our own reality. And yet still, we understand the very human emotions that are at stake. We are both privy to, and emotionally able to, feel as though we are a part of their universe. Even if for just the length of the film, we are let into their world. And of course, that is one of the major functions of fiction: to enchant us into other worlds.

In a snippet of dialogue, the character and personalities of Burns and Hildy are immediately illuminated. We get their sense of sophistication and humor, their class, needs, and desires. We get what I refer to as the "alpha-sensibility" of each of them: Hildy's self-confidence, personal agency, and attention to self-preservation as well as Burns' winsome self-deprecation, authority, and perseverance.

What and how they're speaking might not be the way that we would go about it, but we can easily understand and feel the awkwardness, and we admire the unabashed declaration from a partially culpable Burns of his continued love and affection for Hildy. Most people, especially men, would feel too prideful and vulnerable to openly admit their continued love for another after they've been jilted. But Burns manages to put his heart on the line, which results in the sophisticated tone. So, even though we get that he's a bit of a power-boss, his honesty melts and disarms us, as it does Hildy. He'll do well in life no matter what, which results in the low stakes. In real life, we only wish it were that easy.

What about this from the pilot episode of *Atlanta*, created, written by, and starring Donald Glover:

Alfred and Darius are in the car parked outside of a Chinese restaurant. Darius is eating Lo Mein out of a box. Both are bobbing their heads. "Paper Boy" is playing from the car radio.

                    ALFRED
          (To Darius)
     Yo turn that up.
          (to EARN on phone)
     "Paper Boy". They've been spinning this
     shit for the last hour.

                    DARIUS
     T.P.B. Bitch! Team Paper Boy for life.
          (then)
     Tell em I sketched out them rat phones.

He pulls out a sketch. He takes a picture.

                    ALFRED
     Darius wants to send you a sketch of
     the rat phone. Okay?

                    EARN
     Uh...yeah. Whatever.

                    ALFRED
     Sounds good on the radio. Thanks.

                    EARN
     Trying to be a man of my word.

                    ALFRED
     I feel you. Well maybe we can sit down
     and talk. See if you got any more ideas.

                    EARN
     Like a manager?

                    ALFRED
     Like a "calm the fuck down, we'll see".

Earn smiles. Alfred notices a GIRL off camera walk past the car.

> ALFRED (CONT'D)
> (to Girl)
> Ey baby! That's me they playing on the radio.

> GIRL (O.S.)
> So what?

> ALFRED
> (angrily to girl)
> Well fuck you then! Stank ass broad.

> DARIUS
> (to girl)
> You ain't cute! Fake ass instagram model.

> ALFRED
> (to EARN on phone)
> Yea man, what you doing tomorrow?

> EARN
> Shit. I gotta try to get my job back. I spent the last of everything I had today.

> ALFRED
> (to EARN)
> Hold on. Something's happening. I'll hit to you later, cuh.

Who speaks this way? The characters from *Atlanta*. Is it different than ordinary, real-life speech? Glover has managed to write dialogue that we believe is authentic. Whether it is or it isn't, it *feels* true. The majority of the characters in *Atlanta* are African Americans living in the city of Atlanta. Why are we compelled to listen to this dialogue? Well, we might not be if we were not interested in the life of an up-and-coming African American rapper. But if we are interested, and might even fantasize of embodying such a character, we delight in what we think is authentic banter. Similarly, if we are interested in the plight of a Princeton University dropout who struggles in this urban landscape, as embodied by the character Earn, we might be all the more compelled to watch him survive in what appears to many viewers as an unfamiliar, if not somewhat dangerous, environment.

If we are not African American, or even if we are but not from this particular community, we are suddenly privy to another universe, one with its own sounds, language, and codes of behavior. Such is the power of dialogue, that even on paper, it can evoke its own sense of culture. But the dreams, aspirations, and frustrations that are expressed even in this example of dialogue from *Atlanta* are entirely universal: aspiring to succeed, caring what others think of us, and navigating through each day. From this little bit of dialogue, the character of Alfred is reinforced. He's ambitious, grateful, vulnerable, loyal, and eminently human.

Though *His Girl Friday* and *Atlanta* might be a million miles apart on nearly every level, they are both examples of compelling dialogue that ring true and yet, unless you are a part of the very specific reality of these characters, are not quite like real-life conversations.

In examining the difference between real talk and scripted dialogue, there are a few things to keep in mind. First of all, sometimes there is no difference. Sometimes aspects of scripted dialogue sound exactly the way that people talk, the way that we speak to one another. In real, unscripted speaking, it can be messy, and full of non sequiturs, unanswered questions, half-sentences, single words, interruptions, cutoffs, and pauses. It can also be unintelligible words that barely make sense, or mumbled and misused word usage. It's often ungrammatical and illogical. When real people speak, they often feel the need to supply a lot of information before they actually get to the purpose of their utterance. When real people speak, they use more than just words. They use volume, pitch, timbre, and intonation. They use facial and body expressions and gestures. They use emotional intonations, sadness, exhilaration, joy, and pensiveness, to name but a few modes. It's easy to imagine that if someone were to begin crying or laughing in the midst of speaking, it would surely affect the conversation. It would alter and enhance the meaning of not only the words being spoken, but also of the *intention* of the communication itself. All of this, of course, is also done by actors speaking scripted dialogue. As writers, we attempt to indicate either through specifically written directions or by the content of the words themselves in which way the actors should *act* and should interpret the dialogue. Skilled actors bring nuances and variations that we might not have known even existed.

What is the difference between the function and purpose of dialogue? The function of dialogue is to communicate. The purpose is conveying the intention via the content of the communication itself.

Defining better dialogue

Remember, the concept of dialogue includes speeches, monologues, and voiceovers – all of which will be covered in greater depth in subsequent chapters.

When we consider why certain dialogue is better than others, what examples are we thinking of? For many film lovers, Quinten Tarantino definitely comes to mind, and justifiably so. He excels at both interesting and compelling monologues and repartee. He also knows how to milk tense and dramatic scenes with surprisingly comedic dialogue – made all the more comedic by the violently high stakes that he creates. His ability to have characters speak about mundane subjects littered with pop references in direct juxtaposition to their often violent and very non-mundane actions helps to sear his dialogue into a fan's psyche. A great example of this is in his film *Pulp Fiction* (1994), in which two hapless hitmen are driving to their next assignment:

> VINCENT
> You'll dig it the most. But you know
> What the funniest thing about Europe is?
>
> JULES
> What?
>
> VINCENT
> It's the little differences. A lotta
> the same shit we got here, they got
> there, but there they're a little
> different.
>
> JULES
> Examples?
>
> VINCENT
> Well, in Amsterdam, you can buy beer in a
> movie theatre. And I don't mean in a paper
> cup either. They give you a glass of beer,
> like in a bar. In Paris, you can buy beer
> at MacDonald's. Also, you know what they
> call a Quarter Pounder with Cheese in
> Paris?
>
> JULES
> They don't call it a Quarter Pounder
> with Cheese?
>
> VINCENT
> No, they got the metric system there,
> They wouldn't know what the fuck a Quarter
> Pounder is.
>
> JULES
> What'd they call it?
>
> VINCENT
> Royale with Cheese.
>
> JULES
>   (repeating)
> Royale with Cheese. What'd they call a
> Big Mac?

VINCENT
Big Mac's a Big Mac, but they call it
Le Big Mac.

JULES
Le Big Mac. What do they call a Whopper?

VINCENT
I dunno, I didn't go into a Burger
King. But you know what they put on
french fries in Holland instead of
ketchup?

JULES
What?

VINCENT
Mayonnaise.

JULES
Goddamn!

VINCENT
I seen 'em do it. And I don't mean a
little bit on the side of the plate,
They fuckin' drown 'em in it.

JULES
Uucccch!

What's going on here? Two guys are driving along. In fact, we are introduced to Vincent and Jules by this dialogue before we actually know that they are stone-cold assassins. We can see by their clothing and personal styling that they are prototypical low-level hipster-esque hustlers. And directly after this scene, they load up with revolvers and talk about what they are about to do. But the dialogue feels so innocent and provincial that we are immediately caught off guard and amused by these guys. We maybe even like them. But is this great dialogue? And if it is, why?

The first thing that makes great dialogue is that it is compelling to listen to. Of course, when it comes to judging aesthetics it is subjective and personal. Although it might be difficult to parse Tarantino's dialogue with its specific time and place in film history and its uniqueness of combining abject banal pop culture with extreme violence, the words still work and speak for themselves. Many of its attributes will be covered more thoroughly in future chapters, but immediately, we are struck by the specificity of the language. "Whopper," "Royale with Cheese," etc. Tarantino is certainly a star when one considers great contemporary dialogue writing, but often it is less about the repartee (back and forth) between characters as much as the cool and darkly bizarre world that he conjures and the violence that dramatically increases the stakes.

A terrific example of great dialogue between less extreme types of characters, without the threat of physical violence, is found throughout the film *Juno* (2007), written by Diablo Cody. Consider the following dialogue between two teens, Juno and Bleeker, as Bleeker earnestly wants to be friends with Juno whom he impregnated but who seems to be pulling away from him:

```
INT. DANCING ELK SCHOOL - BLEEKER'S LOCKER - DAY

Bleeker retrieves a book from his open locker. Juno
marches
up to him, belly leading the way.

                    JUNO
          Are you honestly and truly going to
          prom with Katrina De Voort?

                    BLEEKER
          Um, hi?

                    JUNO
          Leah just told me you were going
          with her.

                    BLEEKER
          Yeah, I did ask her if she wanted to
          go. A bunch of us from the team are
          going to Benihana, then the prom,
          then Vijay's parents' cabin.

Juno is clearly AFFRONTED.

                    BLEEKER
               (meekly)
          We're getting a stretch limo.

                    JUNO
          Your mom must be really glad you're
          not taking me.

                    BLEEKER
          You're mad. Why are you mad?

                    JUNO
          I'm not mad. I'm in a fucking great
          mood. Despite the fact that I'm
```

trapped in a fat suit I can't take
off, despite the fact that everyone
is making fun of me behind my back,
despite the fact that your little
girlfriend gave me the stinkeye in
art class yesterday...

              BLEEKER
Katrina's not my girlfriend! And I
doubt she was actually giving you
the stinkeye. She just looks like
that all the time.

A GIRL strides past (obviously KATRINA) with a sour
look aimed squarely at Juno.

              JUNO
Whatever. Have fun at the prom with
Soupy Sales. I'm sure I can think of
something way more cool to do that
night. Like I could pumice my feet,
or go to Bren's dumb Unitarian church,
or get hit by a ten-ton truck full
of hot garbage juice. All those things
would be exponentially cooler than
going to the prom with you.

She starts to walk away. Bleeker takes a deep breath.

              BLEEKER
You're being really immature.

              JUNO
        (turning around)
What?

Bleeker BRACES himself and pushes up his lab goggles.

              JUNO
That's not how our thing works! I
hurl the accusations and you talk
me down, remember?

                    BLEEKER
Not this time. You don't have any
reason to be mad at me. You broke my
heart. I should be royally ticked at
you, man. I should be really cheesed
off. I shouldn't want to talk to you
anymore.

                    JUNO
Why? Because I got bored and had sex
with you one day, and then I didn't,
like, marry you?

                    BLEEKER
Like I'd marry you! You would be the
meanest wife of all time. And anyway,
I know you weren't bored that day
because there was a lot of stuff on
TV. The Blair Witch Project was on
Starz, and you were like, "Oh, I
want to watch this, but we should
make out instead. La la la."

                    JUNO
Forget it, Bleek. Take Katrina the
Douche Packer to the prom. I'm sure
you guys will have a really bitchin'
time!

                    BLEEKER
        (searching for a comeback)
Yeah, well ... I still have your
underwear.

                    JUNO
I still have your virginity!

                    BLEEKER
        (looking around)
Oh my God, SHUT UP!

                    JUNO
What? Are you ashamed that we did
it?

                    BLEEKER
No ...

```
                    JUNO
Well at least you don't have to walk
around with the evidence under your
sweater. I'm a planet!
```

Juno picks up her BACKPACK dejectedly and slides it
over her shoulder. She's about to walk away, when ...

```
                    BLEEKER
Wait, let me take that.
                    JUNO
Huh?

                    BLEEKER
You shouldn't be carrying that heavy
bag. I'll take it.
                    JUNO
Oh. It's fine. What's another ten
pounds?
```

She turns around, wipes TEARS off her cheek (making
sure no one sees) and continues down the hallway.

What is at stake here is the well-being and friendship between smart and likable teens in a heightened emotional situation: an unplanned pregnancy involving two woefully unprepared and too young teens. Their spoken exchange is imminently listenable. Why? Yes, we want them to be friends, but this dialogue expresses numerous levels of emotional complexity, conveying the awkwardness of teens while still being relatable to everyone. And although it isn't purposely comedic, it manages to still be heartbreakingly humorous. *It's able to do this by capturing the unique intelligence of each of them.* Their individual word choices suggest their precociousness and idiosyncrasy. When Juno says:

```
Like I could pumice my feet,
or go to Bren's dumb Unitarian church,
or get hit by a ten-ton truck full
of hot garbage juice. All those things
would be exponentially cooler than
going to the prom with you.
```

It's youthful, vulnerable, and precocious. Between "pumice my feet" and her word usage of "exponentially," we feel that we're in the company of a smart and complex young woman. It draws us to her in an intimate way and we clearly intuit that she feels the opposite of what she's saying as she arms herself with grown-up words and acerbic, biting insults. Similarly, when Bleeker retorts:

```
Like I'd marry you! You would be the
meaness wife of all time. And anyway,
I know you weren't bored that day
because there was a lot of stuff on
TV. The Blair Witch Project was on
Starz, and you were like, "Oh, I
want to watch this, but we should
make out instead. La la la."
```

His surgically sharp memory of "The Blair Witch Project was on Starz" juxtaposed with "you would be the meanest wife of all time" expresses his ultrasincerity in a bitingly perceptive and naive manner. We know exactly how he feels at this moment and we are amused by his nearly random, but still laser-specific, references. He, too, oozes with vulnerability. Their language, word choices, idioms, and pop culture references suggest intelligent, well-meaning, and achingly young people. Their pain is tangible and universal. Their honesty, even if at times obviously veiled, is endearing and vulnerable.

Expressing vulnerabilities requires specificity and deep honesty. Characters *externalizing their internal states through language* is the challenge, and throughout *Juno*, we consistently feel Juno's and Bleeker's inner selves.

We are also treated to a host of words, terms, sounds, and thoughts that are less common in ordinary language and conversation. They stand out like bright colors and stimulate our minds and tingle our ears: "I'm trapped in a fat suit I can't take off," "Stinkeye," "Soupy Sales," "Ten-ton truck full of hot garbage juice," "exponentially cooler," "royally ticked at you," "The Blair Witch Project was on Starz," "Katrina the Douche Packer to the prom," "I'm a planet!" – and all these are in one scene.

Yes, this is superior dialogue: *It is compelling, it has interesting sounds and pace, it scans quickly as you read it, and is intriguing to the ear. It is revealing and raw while conveying complex feelings and emotions that are both specific to the characters while also being universal and accessible.*

In many respects, the way that people speak throughout *Juno* is entirely manufactured; it is the handicraft of a writer. Even smart teens rarely talk this way, and even if they do, they do not do so this colorfully in a single conversation. But, we don't care because it is still accessible, believable, emotional, and brings an authenticity to the characters and their world. These are the hallmarks of better dialogue.

Tone

When we refer to the *tone* of dialogue or, more accurately, the tone that dialogue creates for the listener, we are thinking about the way that it makes us feel. "Mood" is a more psychological term for what we're talking about here. It's literally the vibratory sensibility that we experience, the general attitude. And although feelings are subjective, we can safely categorize some general headings: admiration, adoration, aesthetic appreciation, amusement, anger, anxiety, awe, awkwardness, boredom, calmness, confusion, contempt, comedic, craving, disgust, empathic pain, entrancement, excitement, fear, horror, interest, joy, melancholy, nostalgia, etc.

There are infinite variations and hybrid tone possibilities and each contributes toward the unique way that you feel while experiencing your favorite films and TV shows. Although the overall tone is comprised of numerous factors including visual style, sound, music, editing, performance, etc., dialogue, too, can play a significant part in creating the feel of the overall fabric of the experience. You just have to close your eyes and recall what it felt like to watch *The Godfather* (1972), *Dumb and Dumber* (1994), *The Walking Dead*, or *Madmen* to remember each unique *flavor*, sensation, and tone.

When Don Corleone in *The Godfather* says:

> DON CORLEONE
> Then take the justice from the judge,
> the bitter with the sweet, Bonasera. But
> if you come to me with your friendship,
> your loyalty, then your enemies become my
> enemies, and then, believe me, they would
> fear you.

A deadly serious tone is set. Even if his dialogue is not dotted with memorable zingers, his logic and intentions are clear. He speaks with simple, direct language. Yes, the visual and contextual aspects of this scene are a huge contribution: the henchman standing by his side, the lighting that shadows half of his face, the gravity that Marlon Brando brings to the character. But the way that he speaks is of a piece with the overall tone of the entire film saga. The way in which he speaks is a direct exteriorization of who he is: a hardscrabble immigrant who, out of self-preservation, integrity, and family fealty, clawed his way to becoming a powerful, feared, and revered head of his clan. And tone-wise, we know and feel the precise attitude and sensibility that we now associate with this iconic film.

And here's the opposite tone, from the opening scene of *Dumb and Dumber*. Here, a goofy young man, Lloyd, pretends that he's a passenger in the limo that he's actually the driver of, as he attempts to impress a sophisticated, attractive woman:

> LLOYD
> Excuse me, can you tell me how to get
> to the medical school? I'm supposed to
> be giving a lecture in twenty minutes
> and my driver's a bit lost.

```
                         YOUNG WOMAN
                    (heavy European accent)
              Go straight aheads and makes a left
              over za bridge.
```

Lloyd checks out her body.

```
                            LLOYD
              I couldn't help noticing the accent.
              You from Jersey?
```

```
                         YOUNG WOMAN
                       (unimpressed)
              Austria.
```

```
                            LLOYD
              Austria? You're kidding.
                    (mock-Australian accent)
              Well, g'day, mate. What do you say we
              get together later and throw a few
              shrimp on' the barbie.
```

The Young Woman turns her back to him and walks away.

```
                            LLOYD.
                       (to self)
              Guess I won't be going Down Under
              Tonight...
```

Whether you see and hear this on a screen, or you read it – this dialogue immediately cues you into the world of literally "dumb and dumber." A stupid, "fun"
tone is presented. We know who the character is and we are set up for a similar
sensibility going forward. Is he actually *that* dumb? Yes.

Text and subtext

Typically, when we consider the concepts of *text* and *subtext* in screenwriting
and script analysis, we are referring to all of the information that can be gleaned
in a scene, both implicitly and explicitly. This information is derived not only
from dialogue, but also from a character's actions, gestures, and body language,
as well as any visual/scenic information and context that we can see or is shown
to us. It can also include visual effects, sounds, and music. Added up, all of the
information that is available to us comprises the totality of the scene. When
we say text versus subtext, we're talking about clearly and directly conveyed

information as opposed to information that is not directly expressed, but that is *tacit, implied, or suggested*. For example, we might see what visually appears to be a mild-mannered woman expertly shoot a pistol, repeatedly hitting a moving target. No words are spoken, but it is implied that she's at least more than her mild-mannered appearance suggests. This would be the subtext of this shot. It's not explicitly said, but given what we are seeing, we draw certain conclusions.

When we consider text and subtext in dialogue writing, we are primarily thinking about the psychological aspects of character and how, through what they say or don't say, reveal their interior selves. What they say is the *text*. What they want to say, but don't, is the *subtext*. It's true that in real-life conversations, we often don't say precisely what we feel or want to say. And sometimes, the sense of what we wanted to convey, but didn't say, still comes through. Sometimes this is deliberate, and sometimes it is unconscious. One might want to say "I love you" to someone, but doesn't out of fear that they'd be rejected. Instead, that person might say "I hate you," or "you make me crazy," or "I once loved someone like you," or an infinite amount of things that both convey, even in an obtuse, roundabout, and subtextual fashion, "*I love you* and for whatever reason, I can't say it."

It's what we don't say but what is still understood (if only by the audience) that we call the subtext of the conversation. Sometimes the people involved miss it entirely. It can be completely obvious to an outsider what the true intentions are, but totally occluded to the participants. The value of subtextual dialogue is what it reveals about the character. As an audience, we love to feel that we can see inside a character's mind and heart even more accurately than they seem to be aware of. Even clear, articulate dialogue can suggest layers of specific personality traits beyond their words. When Don Corleone speaks in his clear simple diction, we can surmise his extreme *need* for loyalty and respect. He speaks honestly and straightforwardly and that, too, reveals aspects of himself that are expressed beyond his text.

Some writers and writing instructors use the terminology "on the nose" to describe dialogue that feels inorganically too articulate, clear, and obvious. I've noticed nearly a penchant for subtextual dialogue. Avoiding "on the nose" dialogue becomes a near obsession. I suspect that this avoidance of direct, clear communication reflects a certain cynicism and cover-up for terribly sensitive vulnerability. *The world and people are not to be trusted. Disappointment is inevitable. Only a sap would put themselves out, would expose themselves so brazenly.* Thus, we cover ourselves with misdirections and protective language.

The problem with making direct, obvious language a total anathema, something to always be avoided, is that you forget that some of the greatest dialogue is exactly that: raw, open, honest, and nearly confessional.

Consider this ultra-honest, articulate, vulnerable and *obvious* speech that Beatrice Straight (who won an Academy Award for Best Supporting Actress) delivers in Paddy Chayefsky's *Network*:

> LOUISE SCHUMACHER
> Then get out. Go anywhere you want. Go
> to a hotel, go live with her, but don't
> come back! Because, after 25 years of building
> a home and raising a family and all the
> senseless pain that we have inflicted on each
> other, I'm damned if I'm gonna stand here and
> have you tell me you're in love with somebody
> else! Because this isn't a convention weekend
> with your secretary, is it? Or, or some broad
> that you picked up after three belts of booze.
> This is your great winter romance, isn't it?
> Your last roar of passion before you settle
> into your emeritus years. Is that what's left
> for me? Is that my share? She gets the winter
> passion and I get the dotage? What am I
> supposed to do? Am I supposed to sit at home
> knitting and purling while you slink back like
> some penitent drunk? I'm your wife, damn it!
> And if you can't work up a winter passion for
> me, the least I require is respect and
> allegiance! ... I hurt, don't you understand
> that? I hurt badly!

On the nose? She certainly is not mincing words. She's not avoiding her feelings. As a matter of fact, it's as though her entire insides are splayed out in front of her and her husband. What's subtextually not there? Not much.

There are times when honest, articulate dialogue that directly (and often achingly) describes one's feelings is extremely powerful. Sometimes this is even more powerful than creative subtext obfuscation.

Considering the scene from *Juno* previously discussed, we can look at what it means when dialogue alone possesses textual and subtextual information. Neither Juno nor Bleeker is saying exactly what they emotionally feel inside, even though, in their awkward and naive way, they're trying to. Here, Bleeker is being totally honest and using direct text instead of subtext:

> BLEEKER
> You don't have any reason to be mad at
> me. You broke my heart. I should be
> royally ticked off at you, man. I should
> be really cheesed off. I shouldn't want to
> talk to you anymore.

In contrast to Bleeker, Juno is saying nearly the opposite of what she feels:

```
                    JUNO
        Have fun at the prom with
        Soupy Sales. I'm sure I can think of
        something way more cool to do that
        night. Like I could pumice my feet,
        or go to Bren's dumb Unitarian church,
        or get hit by a ten-ton truck full
        of hot garbage juice.
```

The subtext from this entire scene is that these two teens really do like each other and would love to be with each other, but for a variety of complex reasons, cannot quite admit that. The dialogue speaks to their characters as humans: vulnerable, prideful, confused, intelligent, and emotionally unequipped to handle their situation.

Voice

The term *voice*, as applied to dialogue writing, can refer to the voice of the author/ screenwriter or to the character(s) within a script. When it refers to the author, we are connoting a unique and individual quality that an individual author/ screenwriter brings to all of her work. When we say "the voice of Quentin Tarantino," we are conjuring a specific, ineffable sensibility that he is able to imbue in all of his scripts. This not only includes dialogue, but also content and subject matter as well. When one goes to a Tarantino film, they are expecting to hear his *voice*, or what has become knowns as Tarantino-esque characters (marginalized, ethically questionable, verbose, and eminently watchable) and stories (lawless, morally ambivalent, harrowing, but humorous situations).

There are many fantastic writers that have proved themselves to be extremely agile and versatile in the variety of scripts that they work on. We might not recognize *them* in their script for a comedy or their script for a drama, other than to note that both scripts reflect a professional, high quality of craftsmanship and artistry. Not all writers blaze such a specific trail that they are then identified with a particular style or voice. Tarantino is obvious, and we also equate him with his Tarantino-esque dialogue. Aaron Sorkin is another writer who has a distinctive voice in both his content and his dialogue. When we think of Sorkin, we think of talky, hyper-articulate dialogue uttered by intelligent characters often dealing with serious moral conundrums. This then becomes Sorkin's voice or *brand*.

The other use of the term *voice* is that particular utterance and style that a unique character intones or speaks with. When we first meet Jesse in Vince Gilligan's *Breaking Bad*, we immediately get a sense of the way that he speaks and thinks:

> JESSE
> I don't know what you think you're doing
> here, Mr. White. If you're planning on
> giving me some bullshit about getting
> right with Jesus or something, turning
> myself in --
>
> WALT
> No. Not really.
>
> JESSE
> You ain't "Welcome Back, Kotter," so
> step off. No speeches.

Wiseass, cynical, quick-witted, and contentious – that's his attitude throughout most of its five seasons. Of course, there is much more to him than that; he's actually the heartbeat of the narrative as well, shown less through dialogue and more through action. But he has a consistent vocal *sound* that we equate him with, which constitutes his *voice*. This helps to define him, and it also becomes a touchstone for viewers who come to expect to hear his specific voice when they watch *Breaking Bad*.

Conflict

As different as the various examples of dialogue that we've looked at so far are, have you noticed that there is one commonality they all share? *It's various degrees of conflict.* Dialogue with conflict is considerably more compelling than without it. By conflict, we include any obstacle to any goal that characters are attempting to reach. We are also speaking about textual or subtextual arguments, tension, misunderstandings, disputes, disagreements, discords, friction, antagonism, contention, squabbles, or any other words that describe conversation that is less than perfectly harmonious.

This does not mean that all good dialogue contains shouting matches. On the contrary, considering what we've discussed regarding purpose, tone, text, and subtext, we realize that conversation exposes internal complexities. Complexities often breed contradictions, and anything *contra* posits opposing forces: conflict.

Conflict is at the heart of drama. And to be clear, when we speak about dramatic writing, this includes comedies. There's the saying: "If you see someone slip on a banana peel, that's comedy, but if you slip on a banana peel, that's drama." Note that in both situations, there is conflict, slipping on the ground puts the health of a person's body at stake, and an obstacle, wherever the person was heading was curtailed by slipping, thus placing her arrival at stake. Even simmered-down conflict has something at stake: pride, ego, loss are but a few examples. The entire notion of vulnerability has stakes and conflict built in. When some*thing* is at stake, there is something potentially valuable that is vulnerable to being diminished, lost, or attained. This can include one's self-esteem, purpose, and status. If one is vulnerable, some aspect of herself is at risk. In higher stakes drama it might mean life or death that lies in the balance. But a broken heart or a loss of opportunity can also be enormously dramatic.

Does all dialogue have to have conflict to be compelling? Obviously, if a character asks a waiter for a burger and the waiter says "OK," there is not any conflict, and we don't mind. We are typically not asked to focus on that kind of exchange between characters. And that's fine. However, if the waiter said, "No!" that certainly would be more arresting. You'd be surprised how much dramatic tension, which is mild conflict, exists in everyday talk. Sometimes you don't even realize that you are talking about a rumor or gossip and someone else's character is at stake. Or someone tells a funny joke, but if you look at most jokes they are jammed full of conflict. Dialogue tends to be most compelling when there is tension laced within it, and sometimes tension can exist simply between what a character wants to express (subtext) and what they actually do express (text). But more often in scripted dialogue one character wants something and the other character resists and/or doesn't understand the request.

Exposition

"I am writing this on a computer and I live in New York City." If you read that line in a novel, it might be clarifying, as it gives you information about "me." However, I would never say this to you directly if you were here watching me write, because it would be self-evident. It would be unnecessarily expository. Similarly, if a character gives or offers too much additional information, that either wasn't asked for or is simply inorganic to the conversation, that, too, would be unnecessary, expository dialogue. An example of this is if a character, when asked what he was doing in a candy store, replies, "I was just looking around because my sister lives nearby and I really like chocolate and my father is in the CIA." Aside from this being idiotic, sometimes a screenwriter might feel that they need to give the audience certain information, and in attempting to do so, unnaturally shoehorns it into existing dialogue. This is what I mean by inorganic.

Basically, exposition as a narrative concept in film and TV is a device typically used to give an audience information that isn't obvious or immediately apparent; giving background information about characters, events, setting, time period. Having certain contextual information is important to engage an audience. Without it, we sometimes struggle to make sense of what's going on. And, as could be expected, there is often a greater need for exposition in the beginning of a story rather than later on. However, the need to supply an audience with essential information that isn't otherwise apparent is sometimes a challenge throughout. There are methods to handle this that will be covered in a subsequent chapter, but be aware of how natural dialogue sounds. You wouldn't, for example, have one sister tell her other sister their home address, since it would be obvious that they both knew it. But, a screenwriter thought that we, the audience, needed to know the address and didn't manage to have the sisters speak naturally while conveying that information.

Using an opening crawl, as it occurs at the very top of *Star Wars*, "A long time ago in a galaxy far, far away...." is a classic method for supplying the audience with contextual information. But that is not *dialogue*. It's harder to convey that kind of information with natural flowing dialogue, unless we hear it in voice-over (more on this in a subsequent chapter) or it's being read/delivered to us on screen by way of a storyteller, narrator, speech, monologue, or any number of characters that have good reason to espouse biographical or contextual information that wouldn't otherwise be so immediately apparent. Here is but a snippet of the opening narration from Orson Welles's masterpiece *Citizen Kane* (1941), written by Welles and Herman J. Mankiewicz:

> NARRATOR
> ...Here, for Xanadu's landlord, will be
> held 1940's biggest, strangest funeral;
> here this week is laid to rest a potent
> figure of our Century - America's Kubla
> Kahn - Charles Foster Kane. In journalism's
> history, other names are honored more
> than Charles Foster Kane's, more justly
> revered.

No one would speak this way in normal conversation. No one would state so many facts: the date, the situation, the profession, and the elevated status of someone we haven't even met. But this is still considered dialogue. It's less conversational and more in the realm of speech writing, essays, articles, written material, and professional proclamations. But in a script, these vocal styles of exposition are still considered dialogue, and they have the added requirement of being listenable and compelling, as well as informative.

If we didn't hear and learn this kind of expositional information from some narrative device or disembodied narrator, it would feel contrived and inauthentic. Dialogue feels false, artificial, and pedantic when a character offers or states information to another who obviously knows it already, has no reason to know it, or does not even want to know it. Having a new character enter a scene who doesn't know the lay of the land would allow another character to naturally tell her information that the screenwriter also wants to convey to the audience. This can be a fix that allows one character to inform others about all sorts of essential information for the story to make better sense to us.

The great screenwriter Lorenzo Semple Jr. once said to me: "Have them say exposition when they're dangling from a rope." In other words, when your characters are in an extremely challenging situation they might say the most mundane, expository things: "By the way, I'm a Virgo, what sign are you?"

Expositional dialogue can be tricky. Be aware of how *seamlessly* good film and TV storytelling supplies the necessary information that allows us, invites us, and lures us into the universe of the narrative.

Style

Although in subsequent chapters we will go into greater depth regarding "style," I wanted to round off this chapter on understanding dialogue by including the *notion of style* as it pertains to dialogue writing. What, you might think, is the difference between *voice* and *style*? For now I simply want the reader to be aware that there are styles of dialogue, just as there are various styles of speaking, and there is *stylized dialogue*. Some examples of different styles of speaking would include informal-speak, academic-speak, street-speak, and technical-speak, to list but a few. In a screenplay, just as in life, a character may speak in several styles in the course of a given day. It would be easy to imagine a thirty-something woman waking up in the morning and talking to her children informally as a mother, then delivering a technical, mathematical paper to her peers at a conference as a physicist, and then speaking to a student and his parents as an academic adviser. Here, there are three different styles of speech.

There is also the notion of *stylized dialogue*, dialogue that is mannered, hyper-real, often exaggerated, and nonrealistic. It can also be distinctly anachronistic, from a different time, place, or subculture, i.e., Victorian Era-speak, Cockney, Southern drawl, or Italian mafia.

An example of nonrealistic, but greatly stylized dialogue can be found in *Clueless* (1995), written and directed by Amy Heckerling:

                        CHER
        So, OK, like right now, for example, the
        Haitians need to come to America. But some
        people are all "What about the strain on
        our resources?" But it's like, when I had
        this garden party for my father's birthday
        right? I said R.S.V.P. because it was a
        sit-down dinner. But people came that like,
        did not R.S.V.P. so I was like, totally
        buggin'. I had to haul ass to the kitchen,
        redistribute the food, squish in extra place
        settings, but by the end of the day it was
        like, the more the merrier! And so, if the
        the government could just get to the kitchen,
        rearrange some things, we could certainly
        party with the Haitians. And in conclusion,
        may I please remind you that it does not
        say R.S.V.P. on the Statue of Liberty?

The entire world of *Clueless* is stylized. Everyone exists and speaks in a hyper-real, idiosyncratic manner. Cher's tone draws from the comedic "Valley girl" trope with a brilliant, twisted-rich-girl logic. Although her voice is the most dominant in the film, every character, including her school teacher and her father, are also of a piece with this same stylized universe.

In *Trainspotting* (1996), written by John Hodge, all of the major characters exist within a heroin subculture of Edinburgh. They speak in an ultra-stylized fashion, dotted with streety Scottish colloquialism mixed with a specific drug-culture nomenclature. The main character, Fenton, also brings a brilliant intelligence to this unique universe. Listen to him speak:

```
            RENTON (V.O.)
Choose leisure wear and matching
luggage. Choose a three piece suite
on hire purchase in a range of
fucking fabrics. Choose D.I.Y and
wondering who you are on a Sunday
morning. Choose sitting on that
couch watching mind-numbing sprit-
crushing game shows, stuffing
fucking junk food into your mouth.
Choose rotting away at the end of
it all, pishing you last in a
miserable home, nothing more than
an embarrassment to the selfish,
fucked-up brats you have spawned
to replace yourself. Choose your
future. Choose life.
```

And ...

```
            RENTON (V.O.)
People think it's all about misery
and desperation and death and all
that shite, which is not to be
ignored, but what they forget -
Spud is shooting up for the pleasure
of it. Otherwise we wouldn't do
it. After all, we're not fucking
stupid. At least, we're not that
fucking stupid. Take the best orgasm
you ever had, multiply it by a
thousand and you're still nowhere
near it. When you're on junk you
```

```
have only one worry: scoring. When
you're off it you are suddenly
obliged to worry about all sorts
of other shite. Got no money: can
get pished. Got money: drinking
too much. Can't get a bird: no
chance of a ride. Got a bird: too
much hassle. You have to worry
about bills, about food, about
some football team that never
fucking wins, about human
relationships and all the things
that really don't matter when you've
got a sincere and truthful junk
habit.
```

Here is terrific, uniquely stylized dialogue. It is stilted and mannered while still being accessible and understandable. But most of all, it is a wide open window into the specific psychology of Renton. He's not stupid, he's actually quite brilliant; his logic suggests a thoughtful human soul having wrestled with the fundamental questions of existence – pain, pleasure, survival, and meaning, all the while succumbing to the mournful answer of heroin addiction. This is a voice, a human, a character who, although unreliable in his inevitably drug-addled moments, is also someone worth listening to.

As mentioned, other types of stylized dialogue that are less dependent on an absolutely unique or idiosyncratic voice can be simply characters' dialogue from a different time period, place, or subculture. Here's an excellent example of stylized dialogue from *A Man for All Seasons* (1966), written by the esteemed Robert Bolt. The film, and the play it was adapted from, takes place in sixteenth-century England. Notice its power to conjure the reality of that time:

```
            JUDGE
Master Secretary Cromwell, have you
the charge?

          CROMWELL
I have, my lord.

            JUDGE
Then read the charge.

          CROMWELL
That you did willfully and maliciously
Deny and deprive our liege Lord Henry
of his undoubted certain title: Supreme
Head of the Church in England.
```

                    MORE
But I have never denied this title.

                 CROMWELL
At Westminster Hall, at Lambeth, and
again at Richmond, you stubbornly refused
the oath. Was this no denial?

                    MORE
No, this was silence. And for my silence,
I am punished with imprisonment. Why have
I been called again?

                   JUDGE
On the charge of high treason, Sir Thomas.

                 CROMWELL
For which the punishment is not
imprisonment --

                    MORE
Death - comes for us all, my lords.
Yes, even for kings he comes.

                   JUDGE
The death of kings is not in question,
Sir Thomas.

                    MORE
Nor mine, I trust, until I'm proven guilty.

                    DUKE
Your life lies in your own hands, Thomas,
as it always has!

                    MORE
Is that so, my lord? Then I'll keep a good
grip on it.

                 CROMWELL
So, Sir Thomas, you stand on your silence?

                    MORE
I do.

                  MARGARET
Father, "God more regards the thoughts of
the heart than the words of the mouth,"
or so you've always told me.

                    MORE
Yes.

                  MARGARET
Then say the words of the oath, and in
your heart think otherwise.

                    MORE
What is an oath then, but words we say
to God? Listen, Meg. When a man takes an
oath, he's holding his own self in his own
hands like water. And if he opens his
fingers then, he needn't hope to find himself
again. Some men aren't capable of this, but
I'd be loath to think your father one of
them.

And so we are transposed back in time, simply by the sound and historically specific use of these words, expressions, and mind-set. It's not just peppering expressions like "my lord" into the conversation that makes it feel authentic. It also takes integrating time-specific words ("our liege"),content (kings, oaths, and God) and a manner of phrasing and thinking:

                  MARGARET
Father, "God more regards the thoughts of
the heart than the words of the mouth,"
or so you've always told me.

The power of dialogue to take us to various realms and universes is endless. Great dialogue not only conjures specific times and places, but also bursts with insight into history and different points of view. It takes us inside the minds and hearts of characters, real and imagined.

2

ILLUMINATING CHARACTER THROUGH DIALOGUE

- Introduction: Illuminating character through dialogue
- Character arc
- Outer and inner goals
- Wants, needs, drives, passions
- Externalize the internal
- Putting it all together

Introduction: Illuminating character through dialogue

Every bit of conversation that you have doesn't necessarily reveal who you are or aspects of your deeper self. But it could. A simple "yes," when answering a question could alert the questioner to your state of mind if you, for example, screamed it: "YES!!!" Or if you mumbled it: "Yeghhhhhb." Or if you were barely able to utter it: "Y ... ye ... yeh ... yesss." What each answer actually illuminates about your character is unclear, but something is still going on. It's partly up to the imagination of the listener. Are you disturbed? Exhausted? Angry? Intoxicated?

The meaning of spoken words, then, have levels of information that are conveyed to the listener beyond the actual definition of the words themselves. And this information suggests insight into the heart and mind of the person speaking. The *manner* in which words are spoken can greatly affect both the meaning and the intention of the communication. And so, as screenwriters want to convey various nuances of character, they need to also be able to intimate or literally spell out the way in which they envision how certain words or sentences should be spoken.

The line between how an actor or director interprets the words, and to what degree the writer can control and guide the interpretation of those words, can be blurry. Ideally, the content of the words themselves and the situational context in which they are delivered should be more than sufficient to suggest the appropriate range of interpretation. This needs to be apparent on the page as well as, ultimately, on the screen.

In real life, human sounds, expressions, body language, etc. have an enormous effect on others. We are typically less in control of *how* we speak, especially the nuances and spins we less consciously bring to everyday conversations. We are sometimes unaware that our volumes modulate, or unaware that our faces squinch when we say specific words, betraying some otherwise hidden or unspoken attitude. But mostly, we say what we say the way we intend to say it. But, we sometimes struggle to find the right word or phrase as we stumble toward communicating with one another. This real-life "stumbling" effect can also be conveyed in scripted form. Think of Hugh Grant in most of his romantic comedies as he endearingly, or irritatingly, stammers through his entire role. It's not just what he says, it's the way he says it, the way the screenwriter phrases and writes it out in the script. Using aspects of punctuation, including ellipses, dashes, and single-word sentences, the way one speaks can be conveyed in written scripted dialogue, *and communicate more than the words themselves.* Here's a tiny snippet, written by Richard Curtis, a master of conveying endearingly awkward characters, from *Notting Hill* (1999).

```
                    WILLIAM
     I'm just a complete moron. Sorry. This
     is the sort of thing that happens in dreams
     -- not in real life. Good dreams, obviously
     -- it's a dream to see you.
```

Aside from the hugely important word choices themselves, we can see that the *way* a character speaks, enunciates, and articulates his lines can certainly aid in conveying very human aspects of character. In fact, including content, in many ways the manner, rhythms, syntax, etc. in which a character speaks expresses how that character thinks and how that character's mind works.

* * *

So far in this chapter, we've just emphasized *how* words are spoken rather than the content of the words themselves. And as important as that may be, the content, substance, and language (terms, expressions, etc.) employed will ultimately earn the lion's share of what is most important in conveying the greatest degree of meaning and information about character.

Where do the words come from?

How to choose what words come out of a character's mouth requires a combination of instinct, luck, and an intuitive knowledge of both the psychology of the character and where you need that information placed within the timeline of the story. These last two requirements, *intuitive knowledge of both the psychology of the character and where you need that information placed within the timeline of the story*, can be learned and enhanced. But first, they need to be understood and observed. In Chapter One, we discussed tone, text and subtext, and voice as directly relating to expressing aspects of a character's inner life. Now we'll begin to look at actual dialogue that expresses a character's inner life, aspects that are often unconscious or less conscious to the speaker. When we say "less conscious," we are talking about things that, if pressed, we and our fictional characters are aware of to some degree, but lie below the surface of everyday thinking. We might, for example, be aware of our parents' wishes for us, but we don't think about it as we make decisions that might even be counter to our parents' intentions for us. Then again, we can imagine a person who goes through life entirely affected by their parents' intentions, but is not ever fully cognizant of the degree that they have given up their own personal agency.

In life, sometimes I think that it hardly makes a difference what we say to each other; it's simply the *intent* that really counts. I recall countless times when my mother would call me on the phone and she'd go on and on about something that I couldn't care less about. I was instantly bored, annoyed, and withdrawn. Years later, when I called my own grown son who lived on the opposite coast, I became aware that all I really wanted was to be with him. I mean what I wanted was to literally hang out with him, three thousand miles away. What we said hardly mattered. The words were simply an excuse to take up the time in that awkward, impersonal phone space. My mother just wanted to be with me too. But I was always too busy and too annoyed by her calls about nothing to understand her underlying wonderful, human intentions. And sometimes that would even lead to anger on my part. Sometimes it was almost as though she was provoking me to become angry and irritated as though that was the only way she could engage me in any form of interaction, let alone conversation. But neither of us were aware of what was going on. We were conscious that we loved each other, but less conscious of the ways in which we were trying to express, avoid, or dismiss it.

People play all sorts of unconscious games with each other, sometimes with the most positive, innocent, and pure intentions. Sometimes things are not so positive or pure, but only appear so. Either way, the complex web of communication between people is mostly played out in dialogue. Clear, muddled, and obscured, we, and the characters that we create, reveal aspects of ourselves through dialogue that sometimes we do not realize is so revealing. We might become conscious or even more conscious of these aspects as we evolve, grow, and learn just as our characters might similarly have realizations about themselves and others within their story-journeys. Sometimes not. But through dialogue, we can track a character's progress – their *character arc*.

Character arc

Not every character evolves in the course of a story. But in great films and TV, we follow complex, accessible characters who often learn something along the way. We, too, learn along with them, sometimes lessons that deserve and require repeated learning. At the end of *The Wizard of Oz* (1939), when Dorothy says "Oh Auntie Em, there's no place like home!" the reason it's so memorable and resonant to us is because it's earned. Throughout the whole film, we watch a distressed young girl toil through an elaborate journey all the way to her final realization: "There's no place like home." Her realization is our realization. And it is with this realization that all the imbalances and wrongs of her world are finally, inexorably balanced and righted. Dorothy needs to say those words, just as we need to hear those words, in order for us to also feel complete and satisfied. Dorothy goes through a *transformation*, and so do we.

In screen narratives, what a person does *is* her character. Whereas in prose, we can learn about a character's motives and inner thoughts because the author tells us. In screen narratives, the inner motives and inner workings of a character's heart and mind are displayed by what the character actually does and says. In film and TV, that's what we have to work with: action and dialogue. Just as we watch the physical action of Dorothy confronting the Wizard and feel her mixed emotions in doing so, it is her words, her dialogue "there's no place like home" that lands the full meaning of her personal transformation. She goes from not appreciating the full extent of what she had to deeply appreciating it.

We think of character arcs less in terms of what the actual story is about, and more regarding what psychological, spiritual, emotional, or increased awareness the character gains through their story. In many ways, the story plot is simply a vehicle for our characters to learn, grow, and transform. Action, what a character physically does, conveys reams of information about them. Dialogue, what a character says, conveys levels of meaning and emotion that – together with their actions – leads to a deeply satisfying story experience.

Outer and inner goals

Identifying what a character's goals are helps us understand what words they will say in order to achieve the object of their efforts. When we think about a character's goal, we look for her *primary* goal within a given narrative. This would be the single, unifying object of her efforts, objectives, and ambitions that dominates the actions of the story. Identifying her goals also helps initiate the forward thrust of the narrative, since the concept of goals connotes a future. It's tougher to conceive of what a character will do next if she has no goals or desires. Similarly in life, depression or extreme lack of motivation tends to discourage the forward motion of one's personal story.

That's not to say that there can never be depressed or unmotivated characters. It just makes it more challenging to set them on a course worthy of telling their story. If this is the case, it is often some outside influence or catalyst that enters their stasis, and, like combining unstable compounds, this sparks some chemical effect that motivates them. Sometimes motivation is only their reaction to a new situation that's thrust upon them. But whatever causes characters to be motivated to do anything can be a starting point toward identifying their goal, be it for the moment or for the rest of their story. Conveying to an audience their goals and motivations is a fast-track toward illuminating character. Dialogue can be an integral part of that expression. Oftentimes, the literal expression of a goal is not verbalized at all. But when it is, it sometimes sounds not planned, partially formed, or poetic. Here's Jack, the fallen, former shock-jock in *The Fisher King* (1991), written by Richard LaGravenese, as he works through his pain toward enunciating his deepest aspirations, and ultimately his goal for his entire journey in the film.

>   JACK
>   I tell you something, Anne. I really
>   feel like I'm cursed.
>
>   ANNE
>   Oh stop. Things will change. My
>   Aunt Mary always said, there's a
>   remedy for everything in this world
>   except death and having no class.
>
>   JACK
>   I get this feeling like I'm... a
>   magnet but I attract shit. Out of
>   all the people in this city, why did
>   I meet a man whose wife I killed?
>
>   ANNE
>   You didn't kill anybody. Stop.
>
>   JACK
>   I wish there was some way I could...
>   just... pay the fine and go home.

Anne crosses to Jack and gently touches him. Jack turns and clutches her to him tightly. Lowering his head to hers, he cries...

This scene comes at the end of the first part of the film, the setup. In the very next scene, Jack goes directly to the object of his misery, Perry, and tries to give Perry money; Jack literally tries to "pay the fine." Until the very end of the film, Jack continues to literally or figuratively "pay the fine and go home," redeem himself by helping a person who he feels he's injured tremendously. And in doing so, he hopes to alleviate his tremendous guilt, which would then somehow allow him to return to his previously unburdened self. Unconsciously, Jack, out of great pain and duress, utters his deepest goal: "I wish there was some way ... I could ... just pay the fine and go home." But he's barely conscious of the ramifications of what he's stated. He is conscious that he will actively attempt to help Perry. Helping Perry is therefore his clear, conscious, outer goal throughout the development of the film. But what is his less conscious or unconscious motivation for wanting to help Perry? Redemption. Redeeming himself is Jack's *inner goal*. Jack's inner goal does not only help to relieve his immediate personal suffering, but it also informs his deeper reasons for pursuing his outer goal. Unconsciously, Jack wants more than to "go home"; he aspires to return to some heightened state that only complete redemption can provide.

But goals, like most social–psychological aspects, are complex. Say your goal is to get a good job. But what is the motivation for getting that job? And is knowing what it is the secret to understanding the goal itself? What is the why? The goal of getting a good job is the conscious *outer goal*. The unconscious or less conscious motivation for that outer goal is the *inner goal*.

Perhaps the reason or motivation for getting a good job is to please your love interest. How consciously aware you are of that will determine how much it's really an essential component of your conscious outer goal. If you are extremely aware that your entire reason for wanting to get a good job is to please your husband, then perhaps it would be more accurate to say that your conscious outer goal is to please your husband via getting a good job. This is your direct and conscious goal, and your daily conversations would reflect that. But what, then, would be your inner goal?

Of course, it could be a million things, but whatever it is, it is something of which you are less conscious or unconscious. For example, if your outer goal is to please your husband by getting a good job, then perhaps your inner goal is for your husband not to leave you. And if you were hugely conscious of that, then it would move up to your outer goal, and your inner goal would be the less conscious motivation for why you don't want your husband to leave you.

Do you see that the more conscious a character is of *why* they are doing something, the more likely that those reasons will be expressed through their conversations? And the less conscious motivations will inevitably still come out in actions and conversations, *but not directly*. They will be indirect, shrouded, obscured, and subtextual. So continuing with our example, if the woman is less conscious that her job hunting is motivated by the fear that her husband would otherwise leave her, this might manifest in excessive drinking.

Unconscious motivations don't go away. They play an enormous part in our, and our characters', psychology. When we get to this level of character examination, our characters begin to vibrate with a resonant depth of humanity and luminosity. They also begin to speak in an inspired tongue, dialogue that reflects a character's deepest identity.

Wants, needs, drives, passions

Oftentimes, "outer and inner goals" are considered in terms of *wants* and *needs*. While this can be helpful, there are also sometimes not-so-subtle distinctions that can be helpful in understanding. Remember, we are examining these aspects of character in order to conjure and understand unique and authentic dialogue.

A character can have many wants and needs, but still has a singular goal. Say your character *wants* a Ferrari but she *needs* a car. Her *want* can be her goal, but it isn't necessarily the main storyline of the narrative. Similarly, her *need* can reflect her inner goal as we've defined it, but it doesn't necessarily describe the deeper motivation for the want. Her primary *outer goal* of a story might be to get a Ferrari, but her inner goal, her less conscious or unconscious motivation for her outer goal, might be her wanting to prove her self-worth or out-do her sister.

The concept of wants and needs can still be helpful in understanding our characters, however, they can suggest a host of desires, drives, and deeper rationale for existing. In the case of the woman who wants a Ferrari, how badly she wants the car will determine to what degree her desire will find its way into her conversations. She might, for example, be hyperaware of other people's cars, and her jealousy may percolate through everyday conversations about other things.

In *The Bling Ring* (2013), written and directed by Sophia Coppola, most of the characters are obsessed with Ferraris and their equivalent in high-end clothing. No matter what subject the characters talk about, their preoccupations with the "things" that they want pepper their conversations:

                    REBECCA
        I can't wait to get out of here.

                     MARC
        Is your mom away a lot?

                    REBECCA
        Yeah, she goes on trips a lot for work...

                     MARC
        For what?

                    REBECCA
        She has a chain of student tutoring
        centers...

                     MARC
        And you're at Indian Hills?

                    REBECCA
                   (LAUGHS)
        Yeah, I know, exemplary student...
        That's so cute, I love that dress.
        I love Chanel.

She points at a picture.

> MARC
> Yeah, and the shoes are nice...but
> she needs to get some better extensions...

> REBECCA
> I know, right? Are those Prada?

> MARC
> No, Dior.

> REBECCA
> Really? Hey, what do your parents do?

> MARC
> My mom doesn't work, my dad works for
> a film distribution company, they do a
> lot of stuff overseas...

> REBECCA
> Oh cool, he's in the 'biz'.

> MARC
> Yeah...it's cool. I get to go to
> screenings and stuff.

> REBECCA
> Nice...oh she's so cute.

> MARC
> But enough with the patent leather
> accessories, they look cheap.

> REBECCA
> Yeah, totes...

These characters can't help but express their wants, what they're passionately preoccupied with. Even if the outer goal of the main characters is to rob various celebrities, the obsessiveness of their *wants* informs much of their daily conversations. What, then, is their *need*? Hugs? Greater self-worth? We are supposed to understand these characters as shallow and fame-obsessed products of social media. In *The Bling Ring*, their needs and their inner goals barely surface into the dialogue. Until the very end of their story, they remain shockingly unaware of their deeper motivations. And that lack of self-awareness is arguably the point of the film.

The degree that we understand our characters' inner lives – sometimes even more than the characters themselves – in their fullest psychological spectrum of possibilities, is the degree that we can draw on words, topics, and interests that they might speak about.

Returning to *The Fisher King*, we can see that Jack definitely *wants* to help Perry as the primary action of the film. We could also say that he *needs* to help him in order to feel better about himself. But it gets tricky with the "wants and needs" language, because we can equally say that Jack wants to feel better about himself, or that he wants to return to a state of mind before things went south for him. We can even say that he needs to redeem himself, but again, we can equally say that he needs to help Perry. *The language of wants and needs comes in handy for quickly assessing, with greater depth, characters' various desires moment-to-moment within a story.* But it might be less precise in helping us track their primary actions and their deeper motivations for their overall arc within the whole narrative.

Externalize the internal

In dialogue, it seems easy to "externalize the internal" and one can almost argue that it is nearly impossible not to do it. After all, doesn't everything that comes out of our mouths come from within us? To be clear, when we refer to "externalizing the internal," we are looking at physical or informational manifestations of inner states of being. These manifestations can be expressed through a situation that is a metaphor for a character's state of mind, a visual symbol, or words that hold deeper meanings than what their surface definitions suggest.

To understand this concept, it's easier to look at how visuals can externalize the internal. If, for example, we want to show that a character is stuck in their life, we can show them stuck in traffic, stuck in an elevator, or stuck anywhere. Here, the visuals of someone literally stuck in a physical situation directly informs the character's inner state of mind. In dialogue, especially through the lens of text and subtext, outer and inner goals, and wants and needs, characters also externally express internal information.

Putting it all together

An incredible example of dialogue that exemplifies all of the qualities that we've discussed so far is the opening scene of the film *The Social Network* (2010). This scene was written by Aaron Sorkin, which in part earned him an Academy Award for Best Adapted Screenplay, and depicts a conversation between Mark and Erica sitting at a table in a bustling restaurant. Mark is supposed to be Mark Zuckerberg, and the film is about the founding of Facebook. Other than one of the characters leaving the table at the very end of the scene, there is no real physical *action* in the entire sequence. It illustriously defies the notion of "show don't tell" (the notion that everything that can be visually expressed should be). However, the dialogue itself creates an abundance of *emotional action*, conflict, and drama. Most of all, it illuminates "Mark." It's barely nine pages long and plays out in less than seven minutes on screen, yet it not only reveals levels upon levels of his character and inner life, drives, and passions, but it also motivates his entire journey, while setting the whole story in motion:

FROM THE BLACK WE HEAR--

                    MARK (V.O.)
          Did you know there are more people w
          genius IQ's living in China than the
          are people of any kind living in the
          United States?

                    ERICA (V.O.)
          That can't possibly be true.

                    MARK (V.O.)
          It is.

                    ERICA (V.O.)
          What would account for that?

                    MARK (V.O.)
          Well, first, an awful lot of people live
          in China. But here's my question:

FADE IN:

INT. CAMPUS BAR - NIGHT

MARK ZUCKERBERG is a sweet looking 19 year old whose
lack of any physically intimidating attributes masks a
very complicated and dangerous anger. He has trouble
making eye contact and sometimes it's hard to tell if
he's talking to you or to himself. ERICA, also 19, is
Mark's date. She has a girl-next-door face that makes
her easy to fall for. At this point in the conversation she already knows that she'd rather not be there
and her politeness is about to be tested. The scene is
stark and simple.

                    MARK
          How do you distinguish yourself in a
          population of people who all got 1600
          on their SAT's?

                    ERICA
          I didn't know they take SAT's in China.

                    MARK
          They don't. I wasn't talking about
          China anymore, I was talking about me.

                              ERICA
You got 1600?

                              MARK
Yes. I could sing in an a Capella group,
but I can't sing.

                              ERICA
Does that mean you actually got nothing
wrong?

                              MARK
I can row crew or invent a 25 dollar PC.

                              ERICA
Or you can get into a final club.

                              MARK
Or I can get into a final club.

                              ERICA
You know, from a woman's perspective,
sometimes not singing in an a Capella
group is a good thing?

                              MARK
This is serious.

                              ERICA
On the other hand I do like guys who
row crew.

                              MARK
                      (beat)
Well I can't do that.

                              ERICA
I was kid--

                              MARK
Yes, it means I got nothing wrong on
the test.

                              ERICA
Have you ever tried?

                              MARK
I'm trying right now.

                              ERICA
To row crew?

MARK

To get into a final club. To row
crew? No. Are you, like--whatever--
delusional?

ERICA

Maybe, but sometimes you say two
things at once and I'm not sure which
one I'm supposed to be aiming at.

MARK

But you've seen guys who row crew,
right?

ERICA

No.

MARK

Okay, well they're bigger than me.
They're world class athletes. And a
second ago you said you like guys who
row crew so I assumed you had met one.

ERICA

I guess I just meant I liked the idea
of it. The way a girl likes cowboys.

MARK
(beat)

Okay.

ERICA

Should we get something to eat?

MARK

Would you like to talk about something
else?

ERICA

No, it's just since the beginning of
the conversation about finals club I
think I may have missed a birthday.
(can't get over it)
There are really more people in China
with genius IQ's than the entire
population of--

MARK

The Phoenix is the most diverse. The
Fly Club, Roosevelt punched the Porc.

gue

                    ERICA
          Which one?

                    MARK
          The Porcellian, the Porc, it's the best
          of the best.

                    ERICA
          Which Roosevelt?

                    MARK
          Theodore.

                    ERICA
          Is it true that they send a bus around
          to pick up girls who want to party with
          the next Fed Chairman?

                    MARK
          You can see why it's so important to get in.

                    ERICA
          Okay, well, which is the easiest to get
          into?

MARK is visibly hit by that...

                    MARK
          Why would you ask me that?

                    ERICA
          I'm just asking.

                    MARK
          None of them, that's the point. My friend
          Eduardo made $300,000 betting oil futures
          one summer and Eduardo won't come close to
          getting in. The ability to make money
          Doesn't impress anybody around here.

                    ERICA
          Must be nice. He made $300,000 in a
          summer?

                    MARK
          He likes meteorology.

                    ERICA
          You said it was oil futures.

                    MARK
You can read the weather you can
predict the price of heating oil. I
think you asked me that because you
think the final club that's easiest to
get into is the one where I'll have the
best chance.

                    ERICA
I asked--what?

                    MARK
You asked me which one was the easiest
to get into because you think that that's
the one where I'll have the best chance.

                    ERICA
The one that's the easiest to get into
would be the one where anybody has the
best chance.

                    MARK
You didn't ask me which one was the best
one, you asked me which one was the
easiest one.

                    ERICA
I was honestly just asking. Okay? I was
Just asking to ask. Mark, I'm not speaking
in code.

                    MARK
Erica--

                    ERICA
You're obsessed with finals clubs. You
have finals clubs OCD and you need to
see someone about it who'll prescribe you
some sort of medication. You don't care if
the side effects may include blindness.

                    MARK
Final clubs. Not finals clubs and there's
a difference between being obsessed and
being motivated.

                    ERICA
Yes there is.

                         MARK
Well you do--that was cryptic--so you
do speak in code.

                         ERICA
I didn't mean to be cryptic.

                         MARK
I'm saying I need to do something
substantial in order to get the attention
of the clubs.
                         ERICA
Why?

                         MARK
Because they're exclusive. And fun and
they lead to a better life.

                         ERICA
Teddy Roosevelt didn't get elected
President because he was a member of the
Phoenix Club.

                         MARK
He was a member of the Porcellian and
yes he did.

                         ERICA
Well why don't you just concentrate on
being the best you can be?

                         MARK
Did you really just say that?

                         ERICA
                    (beat)
I was kidding. Although just because
something's trite it doesn't make it any
less--

                         MARK
I want to try to be straightforward
with you and tell you that I think you
might want to be a little more supportive.
If I get in I'll be taking you...to the
events, and the gatherings...and you'll be
meeting a lot of people you wouldn't
normally get to meet.

                    ERICA
            (smiles)
You would do that for me?

                    MARK
We're dating.

                    ERICA
Okay, well I want to try and be straight
forward with you and let you know that
we're not anymore.

                    MARK
What do you mean?

                    ERICA
We're not dating anymore, I'm sorry.

                    MARK
Is this a joke?

                    ERICA
No, it's not.

                    MARK
You're breaking up with me?

                    ERICA
You're going to introduce me to people
I wouldn't normally have the chance to
meet? What the fff--What is that
supposed to mean?

                    MARK
Wait, settle down.

                    ERICA
What is it supposed to mean?
                    MARK
Erica, the reason we're able to sit
Here and drink right now is cause you
used to sleep with the door guy.

                    ERICA
The door guy, his name is Bobby. I did
not sleep with the door guy, the door
guy is a friend of mine. He's a perfectly
good class of people and what part of
Long Island are you from--Wimbledon?

                    MARK
Wait--

                    ERICA
I'm going back to my dorm.

                    MARK
Wait, wait, is this real?

                    ERICA
Yes.

                    MARK
Okay, then wait. I apologize, okay?

                    ERICA
I have to go study.

                    MARK
Erica--

                    ERICA
Yeah.

                    MARK
I'm sorry, I mean it.

                    ERICA
I appreciate that but--

                    MARK
Come on.

                    ERICA
--I have to study.

                    MARK
You don't have to study. You don't
have to study. Let's just talk.

                    ERICA
I can't.

                    MARK
Why?

                    ERICA
Because it's exhausting. Dating you
is like dating a stairmaster.

                    MARK
All I meant is that you're not likely

to-- currently--I wasn't making a comment
on your parents--I was just saying you
go to B.U., I was stating a fact, that's
all, and if it seemed rude then of course
I apologize.

>   ERICA
> I have to go study.

>   MARK
> You don't have to study.

>   ERICA
> Why do you keep saying I don't have to
> study?!

>   MARK
> Because you go to B.U.!

ERICA stares at him...

>   MARK
>   (pause)
> Do you want to get some food?

>   ERICA
> I'm sorry you're not sufficiently
> impressed with my education.

>   MARK
> And I'm sorry I don't have a rowboat
> so we're even.

>   ERICA
> I think we should just be friends.

>   MARK
> I don't want friends.

>   ERICA
> I was being polite, I have no
> intention of being friends with you.

>   MARK
> I'm under some pressure right now with
> my OS class and if we could just order
> food I think we should--

ERICA takes MARK's hand and looks at him tenderly...

> ERICA
> (close)
> You are probably going to be a very
> successful computer person. But you're
> going to go through life thinking that
> girls don't like you because you're a
> nerd. And I want you to know, from the
> bottom of my heart, that that won't be
> true. It'll be because you're an asshole.

And with that stinger, ERICA walks off we, slowly push in on MARK. A fuse has just been lit.

Wow! Here we have a spectacular example of how through dialogue, Sorkin has *externalized* Mark's *internal* self. Hugely important aspects of his inner self are laid bare: his ambition, insecurities, assumptions (some false), myopia, narcissism, vindictiveness, and vulnerabilities. We get an x-ray snapshot of his heart and psyche.

On a *subtext* level, most of what they both are saying is less about the subject at hand – clubs, etc. – and more about the power dynamic between them, as well as Mark's assumptions regarding his relationship with Erica. On a *text* level, it is clear what Mark is talking about: he's trying to enlist Erica's support in getting accepted into the Porcellian Club. He clearly believes that getting in the Porc would be a gateway to enormous successes in life ("Roosevelt punched the Porc"). The subtext is that Mark assumes that Erica is committed to him, and that she would therefore naturally want to support him in his plans. Neither of these, however, is true. Subtextually, Mark also *assumes* his genius and that Erica can't help but admire that in him. Subtextually, he also assumes his future will be monumental; he never says this explicitly, but he has an uncanny confidence about what lies ahead. That is why he is so galled and flummoxed when Erica is not automatically acquiescent. There is a clear divide between his text and his subtext, between what he thinks is true and what is actually true, between what he says and why he says it.

Mark's *wants* are cringingly clear: he wants Erica to be on-board with his plans and to aid him in his ambitions. He also wants to get into the Porcellian. He *needs* Erica to acknowledge his intelligence and commitment to him. He *needs* acceptance.

His *outer goal* for this scene is to get Erica invested in his scheme to get into the Porc. His *inner goal*, his motivation for his outer goal is to soothe his deep insecurities, self-doubts, and self-loathing, and to satiate his burning desire to be acknowledged. And there's nothing particularly untoward with wanting to quell one's insecurities, etc. It is extremely understandable, relatable, and human. We are, therefore, all the more fascinated how a guy with this much mental horsepower bumbles his way through the scene.

The scene is the very opening of the film. Right off the bat, still in darkness and without seeing a soul, we hear a young man's nearly plaintive opening lines, phrased as a question:

> MARK (V.O.)
> Did you know there are more people with
> genius IQ's living in China than there
> are people of any kind living in the United
> States?

Immediately, we are aware that the person speaking is smart, concerned with the concept of being a genius, and a bit condescending by posing his statement as a question. In doing so, the person to whom he is speaking to is quickly put down and made inferior to Mark's breadth of knowledge. In life, certain people actually talk this way, posing arcane facts as nearly unanswerable questions, which belittles the listener. I have known people like this. One person would often contextualize his bits of knowledge by saying something like "As you know, James Monroe was the fifth president, but the third to die on the 4th of July." Actually, I didn't know that (who knows that?) but since he set it up as if I *should've* known, I was embarrassed to admit it, and I let him continue. He, of course, already assumed that I didn't know that information, and it immediately created a strange power dynamic between us: He knows stuff, I don't know stuff. Is this intentional? You betcha.

Consciously or unconsciously, it has a controlling effect. If it's a conscious choice, it might be something learned and copied in order to dominate or control a conversation, situation, or another's actions. If it's unconscious, it might've been a controlling device that one was a victim of as a child, and now uses the same device to offset deep insecurity and vulnerability. When someone assumes this power position, even if they are unconscious of their actions, they still sense the effect of it. For example, as the conversation between Mark and Erica continues, we sense that Mark is likely not fully conscious of his own motivations. Mark desperately needs to bolster his otherwise fragile ego and quell his insecurity about being a nerd.

But he's clearly quite intelligent, and Sorkin describes him as someone "whose lack of any physically intimidating attributes masks a very complicated and dangerous anger. He has trouble making eye contact and sometimes it's hard to tell if he's talking to you or to himself." Is Mark aware of *how* he's speaking to Erica? Is he aware of how it makes her feel? Since by the end of this scene, he does not even remotely achieve what he wants from her, we can only assume that he does not.

> MARK
> How do you distinguish yourself in
> a population of people who all got
> 1600 on their SAT's?

Mark follows up his first question with another, slightly more rhetorical, one. This time, he finds a nonchalant way of letting Erica know, or at least figure out, that he received a "1600," or perfect score on his SAT.

But Erica is nobody's fool, and sensing Mark's power game, even if she can't quite articulate it, she makes a caustic "joke" in reference to Mark's self-denigrating remark: "Yes, I could sing in an a Capella group, but I can't sing."

```
                    ERICA
        You know, from a woman's perspective,
        sometimes not singing in an a Capella
        group is a good thing?
```

This has the effect of immediately sobering Mark up; "This is serious," he quickly replies. But Erica continues to knock him off guard with, "On the other hand, I do like guys who row crew." Erica uses this statement to wind him up, fully aware that they both know that Mark is not, and could never be on crew, and that he uses his brainy nerdiness as his catchall defense.

Now the tone is set and the sparring can begin, but Mark seems nearly oblivious that Erica is a viable opponent. "Are you delusional," Mark quips in frustration, not realizing that she's playing him. And she continues playing him. Who is this guy that is hyperintelligent but can't take a joke and seems unnervingly serious? What does Mark really want from this conversation?

Without having heard what they were talking about before we entered their conversation, Erica fills us in: "It's just since the beginning of the conversation about finals club I think I may have missed a birthday." She is fully in control now, and Mark doesn't have a clue. She may have been textually speaking about "crew," but subtextually, she's talking about Mark's physical insecurities. Textually, Mark has been talking about the population of China, but subtextually, he is talking about his high IQ and how he wants Erica to acknowledge it.

When Mark zeroes in on the Porcellian club, an elite social club at Harvard, it now becomes the metaphor for both Mark's intelligence and his aspirations. Erica, meanwhile, keeps pushing his buttons: "Is it true that they send a bus around to pick up girls who want to party with the next Fed Chairman?" Again and again, she uses sarcasm to fend off his smugness. But Mark continues not to get it. In fact, he's barely listening to her. She continues her attack with, "Which is the easiest [club] to get into?" This renders Mark dumbfounded as he replies, "Why would you ask me that?" The subtext for Mark's response is, "Do you really think that I'm so stupid and inferior that I could only get into an easy club?"

Then, Erica completely levels the playing field with, "I'm not speaking in code," which, of course, is exactly what she's doing. But is she conscious of this, or simply defending herself from being patronized? Mark retorts, "Final clubs. Not finals clubs and there's a difference between being obsessed and being motivated."

Because Mark is so caught up in his own mind, he can't see that Erica is not being serious or sincere with him. Ideally, in a more enlightened sense, he *should* be asking why are you acting this way and what am I doing to create it. But instead, he just plods on digging his own grave by craving acknowledgment from Erica about his superior intelligence and *needing* a crumb of reassurance.

Mark continues to reveal his deepest insecurities, hopes, and dreams in an especially socially inept manner. Although Mark is oblivious, he's also sincere and, thus, he appears vulnerable. Here we see him becoming very direct and textual, expressing for the first time his internal insecurities:

```
              MARK
I'm saying I need to do something
substantial in order to get the attention
of the clubs.
```

Thus, he acknowledges that genius alone is not good enough to get accepted into the clubs. And Erica, in turn, also becomes direct and honest when she says, "Well why don't you just concentrate on being the best you can be?" But she quickly retracts it when Mark trivializes her earnestness. This then dissolves whatever connection they had in the first place. Mark, entirely tone-deaf, doubles down on his "honesty" here:

```
              MARK
I want to try to be straightforward
with you and tell you that I think you
might want to be a little more supportive.
If I get in I'll be taking you...to the
events, and the gatherings...and you'll be
meeting a lot of people you wouldn't
normally get to meet.
```

Erica reacts with complete sarcasm to cover up her anger for being addressed so condescendingly: "You would do that for me?" She then quickly becomes direct and honest when she announces:

```
              ERICA
Okay, well I want to try and be
straightforward with you and let you
know that we're not dating anymore.
```

At first, Mark can barely comprehend this. But he quickly becomes vindictive, accusing her of having slept with the "door guy" of the restaurant where they are dining. Realizing that his approach isn't working at all, he makes a last-minute attempt at an apology. In doing so, he manages to slam both of his feet deeper down his own throat by attempting to justify his previous condescending comments.

As we can see, these are two highly intelligent and educated people. But their emotions and reactions are entirely human, relatable, and universal. Yes, their *class* and education inform their conversation with phrases and content that might not roll off of everyone's tongue, and for those of us who like this kind of repartee it's highly entertaining, but at the end of the day, this is about unrequited affection. Because the story is about one of the participants of this conversation who happens to be extremely bright, it also reveals aspects about him that even he is clearly unaware of.

His insecurity about his own physicality is resonant to most of us. And his tendency to overcompensate with his gift of extraordinary intelligence is equally understandable. He has human feelings and aspirations, but his sense of both entitlement, based upon his intelligence, and some uniquely deep feelings of inadequacy, insecurity, and latent anger, informs his specialness. Yes, we all suffer from insecurities, but how he handles it is specific to him and his complex inner life.

This scene lays bare and completely externalizes his internal self. He's so damn human – all he wants is to be acknowledged and appreciated by the girl he wants to be with. But he's completely out of touch with his true inner needs. Nevertheless, his inner self can't help but ooze out of him, screaming: Please love me! *This is the conversation in so many words.* He's so blinded by his overly bloated sense of self, which he uses as armor, that he can't see what is directly in front of him. He's having a conversation with himself and doesn't realize it. Nearly every word he says, that both of them are saying, has subtextual meaning, which is sometimes the direct opposite of what their words mean.

When Erica finally delivers the coup de grace, we feel the dagger twisting as it enters Mark's psyche:

> ERICA
> You are probably going to be a very
> successful computer person. But you're
> going to go through life thinking that
> girls don't like you because you're a
> nerd. And I want you to know, from the
> bottom of my heart, that that won't be
> true. It'll be because you're an asshole.

When Sorkin writes in his directions at the end of the scene, "a fuse has just been lit," we know that the inevitable explosion at the end of the fuse for Mark, who has been eviscerated and now lies bare and exposed before our very eyes, could only be his own unique explosion. This scene, which serves to motivate him into creating something as grand as Facebook, now makes sense. His outer goal throughout the film is to create what Facebook will become. But his inner goal, beyond the surface level of proving Erica wrong, is to get love and acknowledgment for his intelligence and quell his insecurities.

How well did Sorkin know his character, Mark, before he dove into writing this? I assure you, quite well. Nothing is arbitrary. It's interesting to note that even though Erica speaks equally as much as Mark in this opening scene, it's Mark who is still laid bare the most. Sometimes, another character, even a minor one, can help illuminate the character that they are speaking to. Even though Erica is barely physically present throughout the rest of the film, she sets the tone and the bar for the level of intelligent repartee that follows. She also becomes the object and symbol of everything Mark wants and needs.

It's through dialogue that we understand this entire saga. There are no guns or car chases. There are no punches or even raised voices. These are human beings sparring with words about petty things that, in the moment, mean the whole world to them, or at least to one of them.

3

TYPES OF DIALOGUE

- Introduction: Types of dialogue
- Basic dialogue
- Repartee
- Monologues
- Asides and soliloquies
- Heightened and stylized dialogue
- Realistic/naturalistic dialogue

Introduction: Types of dialogue

I'm not the first screenwriting educator to evoke Alfred Hitchcock's famous quote that a good story is "life, with the dull parts taken out." Even though Hitchcock was referring to the actual story narrative of a film, the concept within this quote can also be applied to dialogue: it must be appropriately realistic or authentic-sounding conversation with the dull parts taken out. However, there are times when we might want to keep in some dull parts in order to create an equally dull or entropic effect, as evident in plays that were a part of the *Theater of the Absurd,* written by, for example, Samuel Beckett and Eugene Ionesco. But this is seen far less in film and television dialogue. And to be very clear, when we speak about "appropriately realistic" dialogue, it is not necessarily the same as "realistic" dialogue. In many ways, the moment that you commit any *speaking* to the page, it is already artificial and stylized. You have lifted words that you've imagined people speak and have written them down. In doing so, you have put a frame around the words and have considered them worthy. This selective process alone suggests that your choices are not absolutely natural and aren't automatically a representation of natural speech. They are only your choices, and thus are stylized.

Rarely do we speak as our favorite characters do. No one really speaks as intelligently and rapidly as Sorkin's characters in *The West Wing* (1999). Who speaks in perfectly formed paragraphs? To say that those characters don't speak realistically is true. However, they speak *appropriately realistically* for the heady world that they exist within. They speak in a way that is still believable to us and in a way that makes us admire them all the more for their nimble, if unrealistic, verbosity.

When we look at the various types of dialogue discussed in this chapter, let's keep in mind that although there are forms other than speaking back-and-forth (such as monologues and asides), conversations between two or more people is what typically comes to mind when we think of writing dialogue for film and TV. But no matter what type of dialogue we're working with, there is a *reason* for it existing at that specific time and place. Or at least there should be, even if the reason is less clear to the characters.

When we talk about writing dialogue, there are really two forces at play: the characters and the screenwriters. Apart from the exalted times of being in the zone while writing, when our characters, like muses, seem to *tell* us not only what to say next but what to do next, mostly, for film and TV, it is the writer who sets the characters in motion. Additionally, it is the screenwriter that knows what effect that she is attempting to elicit in her audience from what her characters say. That being said, once a writer determines the parameters of a scene, its function, who is in it, and where it needs to lead the story, the most pressing question becomes: *What does your character want?*

In Chapter Two, we discussed wants and needs, text and subtext, and inner and outer goals, but these concepts are like fractals throughout the entire narrative when applied separately. In a great script, however, these concepts resonate in every aspect of every moment within the whole story. When we start a scene and ask ourselves what it is that our characters want, the elements that are implied within "want" are *needs*, *subtext*, and *inner goals*.

Basic dialogue

Basic dialogue is the primary verbal interaction between two or more characters.

At least on a practical level, when a character walks into a bar and wants a beer, we don't need to jump through all sorts of Freudian hoops in order to understand why she orders her beer, brewski, suds, wallop, etc. She wants a beer and she asks for it. Sometimes the dialogue is just that simple and straightforward. But remember, we're trying to cut out the dull parts and still sound *believable*. And that is why a more exotic word choice might make an otherwise dull exchange more listenable. It might also reveal something about the character. If your character walks into that same bar and says, "Micky, pour me a *Heiny*," we will immediately know that she frequents this place a lot and she's not a stranger to drinking beer. In this case, it is less about the subtext of the character and more about information that the writer is subtextually attempting to convey.

Here's a snippet of wonderfully straightforward dialogue from *The Shawshank Redemption* (1994).

```
EXT -- EXERCISE YARD -- DAY (1947) 36

Exercise period. Red plays catch with Heywood and
Jigger, lazily tossing a baseball around. Red notices
Andy off to the side. Nods hello. Andy takes this as a
cue to amble over. Heywood and Jigger pause, watching.

                    ANDY
              (offers his hand)
         Hello. I'm Andy Dufresne.

Red glances at the hand, ignores it. The game continues.

                    RED
         The wife-killin' banker.

                    ANDY
         How do you know that?

                    RED
         I keep my ear to the ground. Why'd
         you do it?

                    ANDY
         I didn't, since you ask.

                    RED
         Hell, you'll fit right in, then.
              (off Andy's look)
         Everyone's innocent in here, don't
         you know that? Heywood! What are
         you in for, boy?

                    HEYWOOD
         Didn't do it! Lawyer fucked me!

Red gives Andy a look. See?

                    ANDY
         What else have you heard?

                    RED
         People say you're a cold fish. They
         say you think your shit smells
         sweeter than ordinary. That true?
```

```
                    ANDY
         What do you think?

                    RED
         Ain't made up my mind yet.
```

Here we have about the first quarter of dialogue that comprises the entire scene. It's fairly straightforward with basic back-and-forth *working-man* dialogue. We can't see it yet in the preceding snippet, but very soon after this excerpt, it becomes blatantly clear that Andy's *want* in this scene, or in this case his goal, is to get a "rock-hammer."

```
                    ANDY
         I wonder if you could get me a
         rock-hammer?
```

This is why Andy is in this specific scene in at this specific moment. Andy is asking Red for help, because Red is the go-to person in the prison for "getting things." Earlier in the script, Red tells us:

```
                    RED (V.O.)
         There's a con like me in every prison
         in America, I guess. I'm the guy who
         can get it for you. Cigarettes, a
         bag of reefer if you're partial, a
         bottle of brandy to celebrate your
         kid's high school graduation. Damn
         near anything, within reason.
```

Therefore, by the time that we get to the Andy–Red dialogue, we've already learned about Red's special role, and now we begin to see it in action. In the process, the screenwriter and director, Frank Darabont, manages to convey not only character information, but also world-building information:

```
                    RED
         Everyone's innocent in here, don't
         you know that?
```

We begin to get a sense of what it's like in this prison, the prisoners' thinking, and their moral predispositions. Character-wise, we see that Red is also very aware of everything that goes on. He's smart and perceptive. He is our narrator guide. And although we hear him speak in voice-over before this scene, it's through actual dialogue with Andy that we begin to trust him as a reliable narrator. It's often said that in screen narratives, a character *is* what he *does*. Therefore dialogue in this regard also becomes part of the *doings* of a character.

When Red asks Andy, "Why'd you do it?" referring to the murder of Andy's wife and the reason that Andy is in prison, Andy answers: "I didn't, since you ask."

There's something so calm and nonchalant in Andy's demeanor. Throughout this scene, he consistently speaks in a laid-back manner, which totally justifies the voice-over from Red at the very end of the scene:

```
          RED (V.O.)
I could see why some of the boys
took him for snobby. He had a quiet
way about him, a walk and a talk
that just wasn't normal around
here. He strolled. like a man in a
park without a care or worry. Like
he had on an invisible coat that
would shield him from this place.
     (resumes playing catch)
Yes, I think it would be fair to
say I liked Andy from the start.
```

And, we do too. Aside from Red's voice-over, the regular back-and-forth conversation between Red and Andy lures us into feeling as though we know them both, their characters, their demeanors, and the way their minds work, as well as providing us with bits of information about their environment. This is the potential of regular scripted dialogue, a flowing exchange between two or more characters that starts with a reason, want, need, or goal.

The Shawshank Redemption is a spectacularly good script with passages of equally wonderful, insightful, and powerful dialogue. But we don't remember *Shawshank* for its dialogue as much as we do for its tone and the way the story makes us feel. We also remember the sound of Red's voiceover: soothing, sincere, and wise. Without fireworks and stilted language, the film's perfectly calibrated dialogue rarely calls attention to itself. Most films, including many great films and television, work with basic dialogue that is straightforward, clear and deliberate, and full of text and subtext. It doesn't have to be fancy or super idiosyncratic in order to work. Tell the story with characters who communicate their wants and needs sometimes consciously, sometimes less so, or not at all. Basic.

Repartee

The concept of *repartee* simply connotes dialogue that is witty, heightened, and rapidly spoken back and forth, like a tennis match. Because it is staccato-paced, each side's lines are brief and often only one sentence. Here's a good example of repartee from the noir thriller *Body Heat* (1981), written and directed by Lawrence Kasdan.

                    NED
You can stand here with me if you
want, but you'll have to agree not
to talk about the heat.

                    MATTY
I'm a married woman.

                    NED
Meaning what?

                    MATTY
Meaning I'm not looking for company.

                    NED
Then you should have said, "I'm a
happily married woman."

                    MATTY
That's my business.

                    NED
What?

                    MATTY
How happy I am.

                    NED
And how happy is that?

                    MATTY
You're not too smart, are you?
... I like that in a man.

                    NED
What else you like? Ugly? Lazy?
Horny? I got 'em all.

                    MATTY
You don't look lazy. ... Tell me,
does chat like that work with most
women?

                    NED
Some. If they haven't been around
much.

                    MATTY
I wondered. Thought maybe I was out
of touch.

> NED
> How 'bout I buy you a drink?
>
> MATTY
> I told you. I've got a husband.
>
> NED
> I'll buy him one, too.
>
> MATTY
> He's out of town.
>
> NED
> My favorite kind. We'll drink to
> him.
>
> MATTY
> He only comes up on the weekends.
>
> NED
> I'm liking him better all the time.
> You better take me up on this quick.
> In another 45 minutes, I'm going to
> give up and walk away ...

Rapid-fire repartee immediately evokes a quick mind, a certain intelligence, and a gift for fast-thinking witticisms. However, this kind of back-and-forth banter does not fit all characters. It suggests someone with a specific kind of mental process who enjoys sparring with words and has a predilection toward gaminess. Who speaks like this? It can be fun and light or it can be vicious, but it often masks subtextual sexual tension or more benign desire. Remember, the way a character speaks is a map of how they think.

Monologues

Typically, a monologue is longer than normal speech and is spoken by a character to other characters.

If you thumb through film or television scripts, you'll notice a lot of white on the page. It's not wall-to-wall text like a novel. The directions are usually in short, three- to five-line blocks, and the dialogue, though often varying in lengths, usually tends to not be more than a sentence or two long. Obviously, there are exceptions to this. But occasionally, and certainly not in every script, a character might give a long speech, or a long-winded reply, that's up to three or more pages long! We call those speeches *monologues*. In real life, they happen rarely. But when they do, they are usually long, boring, and monotonous rants by your disgruntled uncle. An exception is if it is a prepared speech delivered to an audience, even if that audience is a family at dinner.

Monologues are much more common in plays since theater, by its very nature, is representational of reality; it doesn't have to pretend to be real. Consequently, characters are freer to speak in heightened theatrical fashions and are able to pontificate in brilliantly constructed language, while still sounding believable within their theatrical world. In real life, perfectly formed, long orations to one another aren't natural. But, plays don't have to appear "natural," since they trade on the magic of make-believe that live performance affords them. On the other hand, film and television mostly trade on verisimilitude, striving to appear absolutely realistic. Film and TV locations appear ultra-real, close-ups show us the pores on characters' skin, and the characters speak in normal volumes and act "real." It is precisely because of this that there are fewer monologues in films and TV. It's hard to insert natural-sounding monologues in a realistic setting that feels believable. But when they work, they can be amazing.

Here are two examples of terrific and effective monologues. The first one is from the film *Pulp Fiction* (1992), written by Quentin Tarantino and Roger Avary. It's from a flashback scene in which a five-year-old, Butch, is told an important story by his late father's war buddy, Captain Koons.

```
              CAPTAIN KOONS
    Hello, little man. Boy, I sure heard
    a bunch about you. See, I was a good
    friend of your dad's. We were in that
    Hanoi pit of hell together for over
    five years. Hopefully, you'll never have
    to experience this yourself, but when
    two men are in a situation like me and
    your dad were, for as long as we were,
    you take on certain responsibilities of
    the other. If it had been me who had
    not made it, Major Coolidge would be
    talking right now to my son Jim. But
    the way it turned out is I'm talking
    to you, Butch. I got something for ya
    ... This watch I got here was first
    purchased by your great-grandfather
    during the first world war. It was
    bought in a little general store in
    Knoxville, Tennessee, made by
    the first company to ever make wrist
    watches. Up until then, people just
    carried pocket watches. It was bought
    by Private Doughboy Ryan Coolidge the
    day he set sail for Paris. This was
    your great-grandfather's war watch,
```

and he wore it every day he was in the
war. Then when he had done his duty,
he went home to your great-grandmother,
took the watch off and put it in an
old coffee can. And in that can it
stayed 'til your granddad Dane Coolidge
was called upon by his country to go
overseas and fight the Germans once
again. This time they called it World
War Two. Your great-grandfather gave
this watch to your granddad for good
luck. Unfortunately, Dane's luck wasn't
as good as his old man's. Dane was a
Marine and he was killed along with all
the other Marines at the battle of Wake
Island. Your granddad was facing death,
and he knew it. None of those boys had
any illusions about ever leaving that
island alive. So three days before the
Japanese took the island, your granddad
asked a gunner on an Air Force transport
named Winocki, a man he had never met
before in his life, to deliver to his
infant son, who he had never seen in
the flesh, his gold watch. Three days
later, your granddad was dead. But
Winocki kept his word. After the war
was over, he paid a visit to your
grandmother, delivering to your infant
father, his Dad's gold watch. This watch.
This watch was on your Daddy's wrist
when he was shot down over Hanoi. He was
captured and put in a Vietnamese prison
camp. He knew if the gooks ever saw the
watch that it'd be confiscated; taken
away. The way your Dad looked at it,
this watch was your birthright. He'd be
damned if any slopes were gonna put
their greasy yellow hands on his boy's
birthright. So he hid it in the one
place he knew he could hide something.
His ass. Five long years, he wore this
watch up his ass. And then he died of
dysentery, he gave me the watch. I hid

```
this uncomfortable hunk of metal up my
ass for two years. Then, after seven
years, I was sent home to my family.
And now, little man, I give the watch
to you.
```

Once you've seen this film, it's difficult to imagine anyone but Christopher Walken delivering this crazy speech. Although it's ultra-sincere, it's equally ultra-inappropriate for a five-year-old to hear. However that, of course, is part of its allure and cringe-inducing humor. As we never see Captain Coons again, this monologue is meant to inform our feelings about grown-up Butch as we sympathize with his younger self. Not only does this help us bond with Butch and give insight into his fatherless past, but it also gives enormous value to the watch itself, which is connected to various plot points later in his story.

The second example is from the film *Glengarry Glen Ross* (1992), written by the Pulitzer Prize–winning playwright David Mamet. The context is that a bunch of desperate real-estate salesmen are given a do-or-die pep talk by Blake, an uber-aggressive higher-up who was sent from their home office to "motivate" them. It's interesting to note that even though the film is an adaptation of Mamet's play of the same name, this monologue was written expressly for the film. I have slightly reformatted it, deleting the directions within it and combining the entire monologue into one contiguous text. Although it's rather long, it is extremely memorable in the film experience, and amazing how compelling and realistic it feels. In this sense, it's insightful and instructive to illustrate, among other things, just how far you can push monologues if the writing itself is up to the task.

```
                    BLAKE
Let me have your attention for a
moment. So you're talking about what?
You're talking about, bitching about
that sale you shot, some son of a
bitch that doesn't want to buy,
somebody that doesn't want what you're
selling, some broad you're trying to
screw and so forth. Let's talk about
something important. Are they all here?
... Well, I'm going anyway. Let's talk
about something important. Put that
coffee down. Coffee's for closers only.
Do you think I'm fucking with you? I
am not fucking with you. I'm here from
downtown. I'm here from Mitch and
Murray. And I'm here on a mission of
```

mercy. Your name's Levene? ... You
call yourself a salesman, you son of
a bitch? ... You certainly don't pal.
'Cause the good news is you're fired.
The bad news is you've got, all you got,
just one week to regain your jobs,
starting tonight. Starting with
tonight's sit. Oh, have I got your
attention now? Good. 'Cause
we're adding a little something to this
month's sales contest. As you all know,
first prize is a Cadillac El Dorado.
Anyone want to see second prize?
Second prize is a set of steak knives.
Third prize is you're fired. You get
the picture? You're laughing now? You
got leads. Mitch and Murray paid good
money. Get their names to sell them.
You can't close the leads you're
given, you can't close shit, you are
shit, hit the bricks pal and beat it
'cause you are going out. ... 'The
leads are weak.' Fucking leads are
weak? You're weak. I've been in this
business fifteen years. ... Fuck you,
that's my name. You know why, Mister?
'Cause you drove a Hyundai to get here
tonight, I drove an eighty thousand
dollar BMW. That's my name. And your
name is you're wanting. And you can't
play in a man's game. You can't close
them. And you go home and tell your
wife your troubles. Because only one
thing counts in this life. Get them
to sign on the line which is dotted.
You hear me, you fucking faggots ...
A-B-C. A-always, B-be, C-closing.
Always be closing. Always be closing.
A-I-D-A. Attention, interest, decision,
action. Attention; do I have your
attention? Interest; are you
interested? I know you are because it's
fuck or walk. You close or you hit the
bricks. Decision; have you made your

decision for Christ? And action.
A-I-D-A; get out there. You got the
prospects comin' in; you think they
came in to get out of the rain? Guy
doesn't walk on the lot unless he wants
to buy. Sitting out there waiting to
give you their money! Are you gonna
take it? Are you man enough to take
it? What's the problem pal? You. Moss ...
You see this watch? You see this
watch? ... That watch cost more than your
car. I made $970,000 last year. How
much you make? You see, pal, that's who
I am. And you're nothing. Nice guy? I
don't give a shit. Good father? Fuck
you, go home and play with your kids.
You wanna work here? Close. You think
this is abuse? You think this is abuse,
you cocksucker? You can't take this,
how can you take the abuse you get on
a sit? You don't like it, leave. I can
go out there tonight with the materials
you got, make myself fifteen thousand
dollars. Tonight. In two hours. Can
you? Can you? Go and do likewise. A-I-D-A.
Get mad. You sons of bitches. Get mad.
You know what it takes to sell real
estate? It takes brass balls to sell
real estate. Go and do likewise, gents.
The money's out there, you pick it up,
it's yours. You don't, I have no
sympathy for you. You wanna go out on
those sits tonight and close, close,
it's yours. If not you're going to be
shining my shoes. Bunch of losers
sitting around in a bar. "Oh yeah, I
used to be a salesman, it's a tough
racket." These are the new leads. These
are the Glengarry leads. And to you,
they're gold. And you don't get them.
Because to give them to you is just
throwing them away. They're for closers.
I'd wish you good luck but you wouldn't
know what to do with it if you got it.

> And to answer your question, pal, why
> am I here? I came here because Mitch
> and Murray asked me to, they asked
> me for a favor. I said, the real favor,
> follow my advice and fire your fucking
> ass because a loser is a loser.

This monologue, delivered with nail-biting perfection by Alec Baldwin, happens early in the film, on page ten. Because of the realistic setting and context, it feels very believable and not artificially theatrical. While reading this monologue, we don't see the faces of the desperately pathetic men that Blake is speaking to, as we do in the film. It is these men that are the main characters of this story. And although we can say that we have a pretty good sense of who Blake is as a man, terribly angry, macho, all-testosterone, uncompassionate son-of-a-bitch, uber-successful, materialistic super-salesperson, he is never again seen in the film. But his dark ethos, menacing tone, and dog-eat-dog sensibility remains throughout. So too does his threat, which motivates the entire story and hovers over the characters like an apocalyptic storm cloud. In crass and vulgar vernacular, his rant informs the brutal reality of the real estate business and serves as a commentary on aspects of capitalism. Because of this monologue, we learn a lot about the men he's speaking to, their values, ethics, and characters, by what they say and do throughout the rest of the film.

As we've seen in these two examples, whereas back-and-forth dialogue gives insight into the characters that participate in the conversation, monologues can also give insight into characters not present in the scene.

Asides and soliloquies

An aside is any dialogue spoken by a character that is intended to be heard only by the audience, and not by any of the other characters in the scene. We see this all the time in theater. A character might literally step downstage, or simply turn and make a remark intended only for the audience to hear. That is an *aside*.

Whereas in film, television, and plays alike, dialogue and monologues are typically employed to push the story and/or character forward, asides are mostly short and tend to reveal private insights, secrets, comments, thoughts, and motives that pertain to moment-to-moment events. Asides are typically just that, a character literally or figuratively stepping aside from his immediate physical position and revealing his thoughts. In doing so, we too are able to pull back and gain the wisdom that distance can give us. Asides, including bon mots, quips, and insightful witticisms, differ from the purely theatrical device called *soliloquy*.

By definition, a soliloquy is a formal speech that characters make that are *intended only for themselves*. A soliloquy is an extended aside that can be similar in length to a monologue but is never heard by another character. It is not intended to push the story forward as much as it is to inform inner character concerns that may or may not be directly relevant to the action at hand. Usually, it is used to reveal deeply mined character truths, existential probing, and philosophical contemplations. Think of Hamlet's famous "To be or not to be" speech. In this classic soliloquy example, you can see why this kind of device is barely used in film or television and is more suited for the stage.

In film and television, the effect of an aside is typically replicated through a *voice-over*. With voice-overs, the action on the screen rarely stops while we hear the voice of either a character in the scene we are watching, another character not in the scene, or a disembodied narrator. And although there is an entire chapter in this book that is devoted to voice-overs, the theatrical approach of us actually seeing a character break the fourth wall and comment to the audience alone does sometimes occur in film and television. And sometimes, it is shockingly effectively.

A great example of using asides in television is the Machiavellian character Francis Underwood in *House of Cards* (2013). Throughout the series, he constantly breaks the otherwise formal reality of the scene by looking directly at us, the audience, and letting us know what's inside his head:

```
Francis kneels down beside the dog. It's in awful
shape. He tenderly strokes the dog's head.

                    FRANCIS
        Shhhh. It's okay...

Francis looks up at us. The sound of CAR ALARM FADES.

                    FRANCIS
              (to the camera)
        There are two kinds of pain. Good
        pain - the sort of pain that motivates,
        that makes you strong. Then there's
        bad pain - useless pain, the sort of
        pain that's only suffering. I welcome
        the former. I have no patience for the
        latter.

With cool-headed deliberateness, Francis calmly places
a hand around the dog's neck and begins to put it out
of its misery.

                    FRANCIS (CONT'D)
              (to the camera)
        Moments like this require someone like
        me. Someone who will act. Who will do what
```

```
            no one else has the courage to do. The
            unpleasant thing. The necessary thing.
```

The dog's muffled whimpers cease. Francis looks down.

```
                    FRANCIS (CONT'D)
                (to the dog)
            There. No more pain.
```

Because *House of Cards* is a TV series, we begin to rely on Francis's asides as a sort of running truth-commentary. As despicable and duplicitous of a character as he is, among a sea of other morally dubious characters, his candor and consistency in relaying the blunt truth to us allows us to not only trust him, but also sympathize with and even root for him. Such is the power of the use of well-executed *asides*. By actually seeing Francis break the reality of the moment and speak directly to us, a Brechtian distancing effect occurs that causes us to suspend our disbelief and bond even deeper with the reality of his character and story.

　　In film, one of the most famous and plentiful uses of asides can be seen in *Ferris Bueller's Day Off* (1986), written and directed by John Hughes. *Ferris Bueller's Day Off* is far less realistic and serious than *House of Cards,* and Ferris speaks to the audience nearly nonstop, almost like a running monologue throughout the entire film:

```
INT. BEDROOM
```

```
Ferris yanks open the drapes. The pall of the sickroom
disappears in the brilliant glow of morning sunlight.
```

```
                    FERRIS
            Incredible! One of the worst
            performances of my career and they
            never doubted it for a second.
                (looks out the window)
            What a beautiful day!
```

```
He turns from the window.
```

```
                    FERRIS (CONT'D)
            Parents always fall for the clammy
            hands. It's physical evidence of
            illness. It's a good, non-specific
            symptom. Parents are generally
```

        pretty hip to the fever scams. And
        to make them work you have to go a
        hundred and one, hundred and two.
        You get a nervous mother and you
        end up in a doctor's office and
        that's worse than school.

He flips on his stereo and fills the room with the MTV
broadcast. A NEW SONG begins.

                FERRIS (CONT'D)
        Fake a stomach cramp and when you're
        doubled over, moaning and wailing,
        just lick your palms. It's a little
        stupid and childish but then so is
        high school. Right?

He equalizes the sound a little.

                FERRIS (CONT'D)
        This is my ninth sick day this
        semester. If I go for ten, I'm probably
        going to have to barf up a lung. So, I
        absolutely must make this one count.

He exits into the hallway.

INT. BATHROOM

Ferris walks into the bathroom. It's littered with
Jean's debris. He turns on the shower water.

                FERRIS
        I don't care if you're fifty five or
        seven, everybody needs a day off now
        and then. It's a beautiful day. How
        can I be expected to handle high
        school?

By speaking directly to us and unabashedly breaking any semblance of what we
often consider "realism" in film, Ferris creates a distancing effect that demands
for us to suspend our disbelief. In doing so, we open ourselves up to be all the
more enchanted by Ferris and his world.

Heightened and stylized dialogue

The term *heightened dialogue* is often conflated with all film or TV dialogue, since simply the act of placing any words in the mouths of fictional characters is already "not reality," stilted, and deliberate. Or it's used as a catchall term to describe any stylized dialogue in plays, TV, and film: mannered, hyper-real, exaggerated, or nonrealistic speaking. Knowing that the key goal for any dialogue, whether unrealistic or not and aside from communicating, is to feel natural to the characters, we can consider heightened dialogue that which goes beyond character stylizations and rises to another level of uniqueness and emotion. Whether it's hard-boiled "dems and dos" of mob-speak, stilted rhythms and nomenclature of cop-speak, or any wildly idiosyncratic voice within those stylized tones, there are notes that seem to evoke a greater, often emotional, resonance. We can aptly call that *heightened dialogue*.

Of course, it is not simply the characters' choice of words themselves that make dialogue stylized or heightened, but also the content of what is being said and discussed.

For example, consider passages of John Patrick Shanley's Academy Award–winning screenplay for *Moonstruck* (1987). The dialogue throughout is stylized as an ultra-romanticized version of Italian-American-Brooklynese. Shanley is an accomplished playwright and the world and characters that he creates in *Moonstruck* lend themselves to dialogue that is stylized with nearly operatic passages that are clearly heightened beyond its idiosyncrasies. I'll leave you with a prime example from *Moonstruck*. In this scene, Loretta goes to invite her fiancé's estranged brother, Ronny, to her wedding. Ronny's a baker, in the midst of baking bread. She doesn't know that he has a wooden hand as a result of an accident, which he blames on her fiancé. Both the content, which is somewhat bizarre, and the emotional urgency render this scene humorous and dramatic. No one in life really speaks this way, but we don't care. This larger-than-life scene encapsulates, in tone and intensity, the entire universe of *Moonstruck*: passion and magic coexisting with the real emotions and pains of everyday life. In this universe, Shanley creates a style and intensity of language that is, although clearly over-the-top stylized, something we seamlessly accept as the natural patois of real Italian-American Brooklynites.

                         RONNY
        Have you come from my brother?

                        LORETTA
        Yes.

                         RONNY
        Why?

                        LORETTA
        I'm going to marry him.

                    RONNY
You are going to marry my
brother?

                    LORETTA
Yes. Do you want...

                    RONNY
I have no life.

                    LORETTA
Excuse me.

                    RONNY
I have no life. My brother Johnny
took my life from me.

                    LORETTA
I don't understand.

Everything in the oven room has stopped and everyone
is watching.

                    RONNY
And now he's getting married. He
has his, he's getting his. And he
wants me to come? What is life?

He picks up the wooden spatula and slides it into the
oven.

                    LORETTA
I didn't come here to upset you.

Ronny slides a bunch of loaves out of the oven on the
spatula, turns them around, and slides them back in.

                    RONNY
They say bread is life. So I bake
bread, bread, bread.
          (He's picking up loaves of
          bread from one of the boxes on
          the floor, and casually tossing
          them across the room.)
And the years go by! By! By! And I
sweat and shovel this stinking dough
in and outta this hot hole in the

wall and I should be so happy, huh,
sweetheart? You want me to come to
the wedding of my brother Johnny?!!
Where is my wedding? Chrissy! Over
by the wall! Gimme the big knife!

CHRISSY

No, Ronny!

RONNY

Gimme the big knife! I'm gonna cut
my throat!

LORETTA

Maybe I should come back another
time.

RONNY

No, I want you to see this! I want
you to watch me kill myself so you
can tell my brother on his wedding
day! Chrissy, gimme the big knife!

CHRISSY

I tell you I won't do it!

RONNY

    (to Loretta)
Do you know about me?

BARBARA

Oh, Mr. Cammareri!

RONNY

Nothing is anybody's fault, but
things happen.
    (holds up his left hand to
    Loretta)
Look.

He pulls off the glove. The hand is made of wood.

RONNY

It's wood. It's fake. Five years
ago I was engaged to be married.
Johnny came in here, he ordered

bread from me. I put it in the
slicer and I talked with him and
my hand got caught cause I wasn't
paying attention. The slicer
chewed off my hand. It's funny
'cause - when my fiancé saw that
I was maimed, she left me for
another man.

                    LORETTA
That's the bad blood between you
and Johnny?

                    RONNY
That's it.

                    LORETTA
But that wasn't Johnny's fault.

                    RONNY
I don't care! I ain't no freakin
monument to justice! I lost my
hand, I lost my bride! Johnny has
his hand, Johnny has his bride! You
come in here and you want me to put
away my heartbreak and forget?

He goes to the big table, which is floured and covered
with bread. He sweeps everything off the tabletop
during the next...

                    RONNY
Is it just a matter of time till a
man opens his eyes and gives up his
one dream of happiness? Maybe.
Maybe. All I have ... Have you come
here, Stranger, Bride of my Brother,
to take these last few loaves from
my table? Alright. Alright.

The table is bare. He stares at it blankly. He wanders
away, to the back room where the flour sacks are kept.
We hear a single sob escape him from that room, and
then silence.

Bravo!! Encore!!

Some excellent examples of stylized dialogue in film and TV include *Clueless* (1995), *Booksmart* (2019), *Trainspotting* (1996), *Goodfellas* (1990), *Sea of Love* (1989), *Pulp Fiction* (1994), *Reservoir Dogs* (1992), *Juno* (2007), *The Big Lebowski* (1998), *In Bruges* (2008), *The Wire* (2002), *Deadwood* (2004), *True Detective* (Season One), *The Sopranos* (1999), and *The West Wing* (1999).

Realistic/naturalistic dialogue

In discussing various types of dialogue from the ordinary to the extraordinary, we've noted that all dialogue, by its very nature of being fiction, is "not real." There is, however, something called realistic or naturalistic dialogue. This is dialogue that specifically aspires to sound and feel as authentic and realistic as possible. It is dialogue that, in fact, is derived directly from actual natural speech or attempts to imitate it very closely. To get an idea of how untenable actual dialogue would be in scripted narratives, consider what the transcript from any interview or real conversation might be like: long-winded, boring, full of pauses (for thinking or cigarette puffs and coughs), "ers" and "ums," repetitions, incorrect word usage, awkward correction of vocab mistakes, or rethinking of new sentences, etc. It is not that it's impossible to transpose unedited natural speech into scripted narratives, as much as it is not functional nor efficient, and is ungainly and harder to sculpt into compelling passages and scenes.

Nevertheless, knowing that absolutely natural and realistic speech isn't ever entirely possible, certain screenwriters tend to make their characters speak in ways that still feel very real and authentic. It's no wonder that some of the films whose dialogue we consider so realistic come from on-set improvisations. Much of the mumblecore films share this naturalist style and feeling. Writer-directors like Mike Leigh, Woody Allen, Joe Swanberg, Richard Linklater, and Noah Baumbach excel at mimicking what we consider real-sounding dialogue. Like in real life, their characters might talk over each other, speak in non sequiturs, and leave sentences unfinished with unexpected pauses.

Here's part of the opening scene from Noah Baumbach's film *The Meyerowitz Stories* (2017):

```
INT. DANNY'S SUBARU OUTBACK. DAY

Danny Meyerowitz, mid-40's, is backing up on the
Bowery. He wears a soft brown leather jacket and
shorts. Eliza, his 18 year old daughter, is flipping
channels on the radio.

                    ELIZA
        I'm really thinking about being
        vegetarian again.
```

                    DANNY
          Eliza--

                    ELIZA
          Do you realize, eating meat is
          worse than driving an SUV for a
          year.

                    DANNY
          Eliza, am I fitting?

A car honks.

                    DANNY
          I'm parking asshole!
               (twisting the wheel)
          I can't believe that's true.

                    ELIZA
          It's true, Dad. I'll send you
          the Podcast.

                    DANNY
          I don't think I'm fitting.

                    ELIZA
          I'm telling you. It's a big
          thing we can do for the
          environment.

                    DANNY
          Let's look it up. But not while
          I'm pulling THIS maneuver.

He turns the wheel dramatically. There's a scraping
sound followed by a thud.

                    ELIZA
          It's too small a space.

                    DANNY
          Shit!

He shifts back into drive and pulls out into traffic.
More horns.

                    DANNY
               (to the car behind him)
          What?!

Eliza fiddles with the radio, looking for a song.

>   DANNY
>   Go back to the Mets game.

>   ELIZA
>   It's a commercial.

>   DANNY
>   I splurged and got the satellite.

She lands on "Head to Toe" by Lisa Lisa and the Cult
Jam.

>   DANNY
>   Ooh, nice. Turn it up.

Eliza turns up the song.

>   DANNY
>   "Head to toe --"
>   (cutting himself off)
>   I put this on a tape for you
>   when you were like twelve.

>   ELIZA
>   (mildly interested)
>   Cool.

Danny looks over his shoulder, realizes something, and
hits the wheel in frustration.

>   DANNY
>   Shit, was that ... was that a
>   spot?

>   ELIZA
>   (looking back)
>   Yeah, he's taking it.

>   DANNY
>   How did I miss that? Fucking
>   shit.

>   ELIZA
>   Let's go around.

You get the idea. It's chaotic, unruly, and spontaneous, like reality.

Most film and TV dialogue aspires to be believable, at least within the construct of the particular character. And many great films and TV shows are great without particularly memorable dialogue per se. But dialogue that evokes in us a certain recognition that "I've had that conversation," warts and all, we can categorize as realistic or naturalistic dialogue.

4

VOICE-OVERS AND NARRATIONS

Introduction: Voice-overs and narrations

Beyond any narrative and/or character-building function (adding or spinning information), a major aspect to consider regarding the entire topic of voice-over and narration is how it affects the emotional tone of a given narrative and how it makes the audience feel. In this chapter, we will discuss different types of voice-overs, their function and purpose, and identify some of the hows and whys voice-overs contribute to the creation of a memorable visual narrative experience.

* * *

I can only speculate as to why this is, but whenever the concept of "voice-over" is spoken about in the writing of film and television, there is always a cadre of people who seem to have a knee-jerk reaction against it. Some of these dislikers will automatically regurgitate tropes that they have been taught along the way, like "show don't tell!" in some smug, hipster-militaristic manner. It's even satirized in the film *Adaptation* (2002), when the film guru Robert McKee, played by Brian Cox, says: "God help you if you use voice-over in your work, my friends. God help you. That's flaccid, sloppy writing. Any idiot can write a voice-over narration to explain the thoughts of a character."

As has been previously discussed, this "show don't tell" notion is generally a truthful and wise adage for most descriptive writing – and it should be especially considered when writing for screen narratives. This should be obvious because in screen narratives, we are working in a visual medium. Whether via voice-over technique or normal dialogue, there will always be cineastes out there who favor a minimal-to-no-dialogue film experience, often touting the virtues of *pure*, visual cinema. Needless to say, I am not among them. Silent films, without a doubt, have their place, especially in film history. That place was before 1927, when the first "talky" film, *The Jazz Singer* (1927), came out. It all changed after that.

No matter where you stand on the use of voice-overs, when asked to list your top ten favorite films, it's amazing how often that north of fifty percent of the list contains films that employ voice-overs.

To name but a few great films that use voice-over techniques: *The Shape of Water* (2017), *Stand by Me* (1986), *Memento* (2000), *500 Days of Summer* (2009), *Citizen Kane* (1941), *Sunset Boulevard* (1950), *Amelie* (2001), *The Royal Tenenbaums* (2001), *Apocalypse Now* (1979), *The Big Lebowski* (1998), *To Kill a Mockingbird* (1962), *Goodfellas* (1990), *The Third Man* (1949), *The Princess Bride* (1987), *Trainspotting* (1996), *Annie Hall* (1977), *Taxi Driver* (1976), *Jules and Jim* (1962), *Fight Club* (1999), *The Shawshank Redemption* (1994), *American Beauty* (1999), *Badlands* (1973), *The Usual Suspects* (1995), *Life of Pi* (2012), *Casino* (1995), *Big Fish* (2003), *Heathers* (1988), *Clockwork Orange* (1971), *The Social Network* (2010), *American Psycho* (2000), *Adaptation* (2002), *Stranger than Fiction* (2006), *The Big Short* (2015), *Fear and Loathing in Las Vegas* (1998), *Double Indemnity* (1944), *All About Eve* (1950), *Kiss Kiss Bang Bang* (2005), and *Raising Arizona* (1987).

A few memorable television shows: *Mr. Robot*, *House of Cards*, *Arrested Development*, *Veronica Mars*, *Burn Notice*, *Ally McBeal*, *The Mindy Project*, *Felicity*, *Jane the Virgin*, *My So-Called Life*, *The Wonder Years*, *Ugly Betty*, *Pushing Daisies*, *My Name Is Earl*, *Desperate Housewives*, *Grey's Anatomy*, *How I Met Your Mother*, *Gossip Girl*, *Everybody Hates Chris*, *Sex and the City*, *Dexter*, *Veronica Mars*, *Scrubs*, and *The Goldbergs*.

So, what is it?

The term "voice-over," "(V.O.)," or "NARRATOR," as it is commonly seen next to a character's name on a script, simply means that we hear the voice speaking, but do not see the person speaking; the narrator is not physically present in the visual reality of the scene. We may be watching a character and hear in voice-over that same character comment on the scene, or even on herself. But, that person or voice that we hear may or may not ever be seen physically in any scene in the entire narrative. Or possibly, they are seen very briefly, without a significant role to play – as with Sam Elliot's The Stranger's voice-over in *The Big Lebowski*. Or, we might see a character on screen and then hear her voice spoken from another time frame, often from a future time in her life, and never see that character at the age of her narration. This can be seen in "Scout's" older self in *To Kill a Mockingbird*. We see Scout as a child, but hear her as an adult looking back, and we never see her at the age that she is speaking from. And that, too, would be a voice-over or narration.

Sometimes, this voice-over takes the form of a disembodied voice that does not belong to a character from within the narrative. This voice is simply a storyteller, someone that guides us through the story either continuously and/or periodically shows up, *in voice only*, at various times within the narrative. Two examples of this are *Amelie* and *The Magnificent Ambersons* (1942).

Then there is the kind of voice-over or narration that closely knits the character speaking with the story itself. Sometimes we come to learn that the voice-over has a specific purpose and/or it is actual dialogue from a future scene that has not arrived yet. We might learn, for example, that what we've been hearing is in fact an interview with a psychologist, an interrogation with the police, a speech being delivered, or a book that's being read aloud or spoken aloud while being written. We often learn this information at a key point in the story, commonly at the very end, but sometimes at the midpoint or the end of act two.

Although conventional wisdom suggests that the content of the voice-over should add something to a scene beyond what we can see, this isn't always the case, as we'll see in some upcoming examples. But for the most part, voice-over/narration should expand and illuminate our understanding of the character, story, or both – beyond what we see or learn from the scene alone. As we investigate this further, we'll examine numerous usages and variations of voice-overs. And most important, what we gain from it, not only informationally but also emotionally.

Structure markers

Although there are some films in which voice-overs are heard randomly throughout, often voice-overs serve as structural markers within the narrative. It's quite typical, for example, to place a voice-over at various key locations within the narrative, such as the beginning (setting the tone), the end of act one (reinforcing the setup), at the midpoint (denoting a shift of tone, character, or time/place), the end of act two (heightening the conflict and setting up the inevitable climax), and at the very end (to summarize and/or create a satisfying coda on the story).

* * *

Asides and soliloquies

In live theater, when a character wants to do the equivalent of a film voice-over, it is called an *aside*. It's a dramatic device in which a character speaks directly to the audience while the other characters on the stage do not hear him. In this case, a character might simply step forward to tell the audience additional information, comment on a character, or give context beyond what is known or gleaned so far in the play. Sometimes a character might even step in front of a closed curtain and speak to the audience, voicing her own thoughts aloud, as if to herself. We call that a *soliloquy*. The word "soliloquy" is derived from the Latin roots *solus* ("alone") and *loqui* ("speak"). Together, this means: "a talking to oneself."

In screen narratives, film and TV, we rarely hear soliloquies or inner monologues as simply voice-overs without also seeing the speaker actually speaking. Sometimes, during more self-reflective passages, it is effective to intercut between the emotional face of the speaker (actually speaking or not) and other images that strive to further externalize her interior life. Since the power of screen narratives often relies on its verisimilitude and ability to mimic reality, it is less common to see a character break the fourth wall and speak directly to us within a scene. Instead, we usually only hear voice-over or narration as the equivalent of a theatrical aside or soliloquy. There are some exceptions, such as *Ferris Bueller's Day Off* (1986), in which Ferris basically speaks *asides* directly to the audience all throughout the film. A variation of this is seen in *Memento* when the main character, Leonard, who suffers from amnesia, speaks to himself in voice-over; we hear what he's thinking about as he's thinking about it. We hear his own private, inner thoughts to himself. He is not speaking to us, the audience. Instead, he is speaking in his mind and occasionally aloud, only to himself. If we saw him on stage playing this part, his voice-overs from the film would appear as a kind of live-running soliloquy.

Often, the function of narration that we only hear while watching a scene or a transitional scene is to do exactly what some of its detractors get in a tizzy about: *it tells without showing*. It conveys to us, the audience, information that we don't see. This information is about a character's past, present, and future. Or, it is about the world of the story, much the same way that a novelist can describe what is inside the mind of characters, or even comment about a character or aspects of the story itself. In doing so, voice-over narration can compress years and reams worth of information that we otherwise wouldn't see, which would take hours to "show" if it were integrated into the story. It could also direct our attention to large amounts, or tiny nuanced bits, of information that would simply be impossible to convey with visuals alone without some sort of explanation through actual dialogue. In *Stand by Me*, the narrator, Gordie Lachance, is one of our main characters looking back from adulthood at a specific episode of his life. As we see and meet his friends, he adds additional information that his younger self may or may not have been entirely conscious of, regarding his best friend Chris:

```
            NARRATOR (V.O.)
    (Adult Gordon)
    Chris was the leader of our gang,
    and my best friend. He came from
    a bad family and everybody thought
    he would turn out bad ... including Chris.
```

The use of voice-over in *Stand by Me* perfectly illustrates many of the positive attributes that come from purposeful narration. In the preceding example, which comes at the beginning of the film, we hear Gordie's older self (Gordon) comment about his friends. We then watch him and his friends in their treehouse as kids. We might possibly glean that Chris was his "best friend" when watching the scene, though it certainly isn't obvious. We definitely would not get that Chris "came from a bad family and everyone thought that he'd turn out bad ... including Chris," from this scene. In fact, it is not until much later in the story that we will learn aspects of this as we watch Chris and Gordie interact in, by then, an emotionally earned scene. But by letting us know this information right off the bat, it guides us toward an emotional response to Chris and Gordie's relationship that we would not otherwise feel. From this point on, we view Chris through the lens of this otherwise unseen information. It helps us bond with Chris just as it helps us trust the young Gordie.

As this example points out, there is something huge and important beyond the technical and functional aspects of various voice-overs: voice-overs can affect the tone of the story. This aspect cannot be undervalued, as it is often a major contributor to how we *feel* about a film. Can you imagine not hearing Morgan Freeman's voice throughout *The Shawshank Redemption*? I can't.

There is something that is singularly cozy and comforting about having a story read aloud to you. Whether we associate this with our parents reading stories to us before we went to bed, the sensation of listening to a radio play while lounging on the couch, or hearing a spooky tale around a campfire, there seems to be some nearly neurological comfort in the act of listening to a story. Most every religion is replete with oral recitations of liturgies, mythologies, legends, and tales. It is as though humans have a built-in need to have stories told to them.

It is the "once upon a time" magic that comes with voice-over narration that is essential. As a writer, you need to ask yourself if you want to conjure this particular feeling for your audience.

Emotionality

What is this *feeling* that is conjured through narration? It is often full of nostalgia, melancholy, and longing. Sometimes, it conveys wry intelligence or emotions that are not otherwise able to be as explicitly conveyed visually without a voice-over. A friendly, benign narration can make us feel safe or secure even when the images, events, and music suggest otherwise; we "know" that the person speaking will survive and will not die by the end of the story. Or so we think. We learn otherwise, right from the beginning in *Sunset Boulevard* and *American Beauty*. It's interesting to note that in both of these films, the choice by the filmmakers to hear a dead person speaking throughout (and to show him dead in the beginning of *Sunset Boulevard*) was not part of their original scripts. But by hearing their voice-over narrate from beyond the grave makes us, the audience, co-conspirators in the fantasy of being able to speak after dying. It also makes the inherently dark tone feel lighter. It makes a tragedy accessible, palatable. Consider when Lester Burnham talks to us in voice-over, after his death at the end of *American Beauty*:

> LESTER (V.O.)
> I had always heard your entire life
> flashes in front of your eyes the
> second before you die.

EXT. SKY - DAY

We're FLYING across a white blanket of clouds.
(NOTE: THERE ARE VISUALS REPRESENTING WHAT LESTER SAYS
THAT ARE NOT INCLUDED BELOW)

> LESTER (V.O.)
> First of all, that one second isn't
> a second at all, it stretches on
> forever, like an ocean of time ...
> For me, it was lying on my back at
> Boy Scout camp, watching falling
> Stars ... And yellow leaves,
> from the maple trees, that lined
> my street ...
> Or my grandmother's hands, and the
> way her skin seemed like paper ...
> And the first time I saw my cousin
> Tony's brand new Firebird ...
> And Janie ...
> And Janie...
>   (with love)
> And... Carolyn. ...
> I guess I could be pretty pissed off
> about what happened to me ... but it's
> hard to stay mad, when there's so
> much beauty in the world. Sometimes
> I feel like I'm seeing it all at once,

```
              and it's too much, my heart fills up
              like a balloon that's about to burst ...
              ... and then I remember to relax, and
              stop trying to hold on to it, and then
              it flows through me like rain and I
              can't feel anything but gratitude for
              every single moment of my stupid
              little life ...
                        (amused)
              You have no idea what I'm talking
              about, I'm sure. But don't worry ...

FADE TO BLACK:
                        LESTER (V.O.)
              You will someday.
                        THE END
```

Wow! For those of us who like this film, this is perfect. It is very easy for me to imagine *not* feeling as good about life, Lester, and the whole experience of watching *American Beauty* without this voice-over. Without this voice-over, ironic or not, I'd feel depressed and overwhelmed by the burdens of this American tragedy. It might be possible to construct an ending without Lester's voice-over and still get me to feel this philosophically effervescent, nearly transcendent feeling, but ... highly unlikely.

Is it a boldface manipulation? Is it an effect to sugar-coat or lessen the blow? Is it a cop-out? Sure, narrations can be all of these things or their opposites. It is a powerful tool, technique, and device.

Literary dimension

Voice-overs add a literary dimension to a narrative. Prose fiction usually employs a combination of third-person storytelling and first-person storytelling by way of its dialogue to guide the reader through its narratives. Third-person storytelling is unto itself a voice-over without calling attention to itself. It's the "voice" of the author or an assumed character telling the story. In prose, the author, either through a character or her own voice, *tells* us about the world of the story and what the characters are feeling and thinking. Often, the author tells us how we, the reader, should interpret their given information. Among voice-over detractors, this is exactly what they have against this device in films – they consider voice-overs a device that undermines an audience's ability to absorb the narrative by explicitly telling them what to think or feel.

I suggest that, although that might be true in some cases, on balance, what you gain with appropriate voice-over more than justifies its usage. Again, it also goes back to that primal sense of having someone reading you a story. Not only is the "once upon a time" a great beginning toward setting the parameters of the experience, but so too is "and they all lived happily ever after" an equally satisfying and comforting ending. Both can be spoken by a never-identified voice within the actual story itself.

A hallmark of good prose or literature is that through language, an author can dig deep into a character's psyche and/or illuminate dense complexities. Oftentimes, the poetry of language alone is what separates it from ever being visually represented. By using authorial language in voice-over, it not only gives us the distance of third-person prose, but it also combines literary ideas and languages with the visuals of cinema. Combined, this can generate a magical effect.

In *American Beauty*, we don't *see* Lester "alive" at the end, we only hear him. This, of course, implies that Lester exists in some incorporeal state and therefore remains alive in our imagination as we leave the theater or finish watching his story. The suburban horrors, the pedophilia; sexual, spousal, and child abuse; and infidelity within the film are, if not wiped under the table, actually made all the more … palatable. This gives us, the audience, literary distance to ponder and process the story, characters, and themes into our own psyches. Something that we similarly tend to do with literature and the act of reading itself.

Perhaps it is this sense of distance and explicit "make-believe" that voice-overs conjure that allow us to, like children, more easily suspend our disbelief and collaborate with the fiction. Voice-overs typically intrude upon a visual reality, reminding us that what we're seeing is not reality, but a story being presented. A voice-over calls attention not only to itself, but also to the entire narrative construction, the tone and rules of the complete universe of the story. The voice-over reminds us that we are being told a story … by someone.

By whom?

* * *

The three basic types of voice-over

There are three general types of voice-over: the voice of God, looking back, and part of the story. Within these three categories there are often crossovers and hybrids.

The voice-of-God V.O.

An anonymous, omniscient narrator...

This is the omniscient *narrator*, an anonymous voice, the *storyteller*. It could be a cynical or manipulative incorporeal point of view or a wise, good-natured, friendly voice conveying a safe and secure tone. The voice of God is the voice that says "once upon a time …" Who is this voice? It's the voice of the God who hovers over the story.

Although this anonymous voice-of-God-style narrator is still used today, it was more popular in the past. From the beginning of "talkies" well into the '50s, the voice of God, or an anonymous, omniscient narrator was fairly common. Often, this was because many of the films were from novels and plays and the voice-over narrator device was the best attempt to replicate and stay true to the tone and nature of the adapted source material. One could argue that we still adapt many novels and plays, but without using the "narrator" device as frequently. I might suggest that the concept of auteurism – in which the director is considered the primary creative force in a motion picture – gained expanding relevance starting in the late 1940s. Since then, many filmmakers have increasingly striven to create greater sunlight between the source material and their finished creations.

Consider the opening of *The Magnificent Ambersons*, the 1942 film nominated for four Academy Awards, and directed and written by the fiercely auteurist Orson Welles. It was adapted by Welles from the 1918 Pulitzer Prize–winning novel by Booth Tarkington of the same name. Note: Welles also used his own voice as the narrator in his film.

```
                    NARRATOR
     The magnificence of the Ambersons began
     in 1873. Their splendor lasted
     throughout all the years that saw their
     Midland town spread and darken into a
     City ... In that town in those days,
     all the women who wore silk or velvet
     knew all the other women who wore silk
     or velvet ---- and everybody knew
     everybody else's family horse-and-
     carriage.
```

And this is the opening of the novel by Booth Tarkington:

Major Amberson had "made a fortune" in 1873, when other people were losing fortunes, and the magnificence of the Ambersons began then. Magnificence, like the size of a fortune, is always comparative, as even Magnificent Lorenzo may now perceive, if he has happened to haunt New York in 1916; and the Ambersons were magnificent in their day and place. Their splendour lasted throughout all the years that saw their Midland town spread and darken into a city, but reached its topmost during the period when every prosperous family with children kept a Newfoundland dog. In that town, in those days, all the women who wore silk or velvet knew all the other women who wore silk or velvet, and when there was a new purchase of sealskin, sick people were got to windows to see it go by.

There are infinite ways to compress and interpret Tarkington's opening prose into the film narrator's opening tongue. Welles, who was as "auteur" as any filmmaker in history, was still confident enough to maintain the voice, tone, and integrity of the novel that had been popular two decades earlier.

Aside from the written word, we must take into account that Welles's own voice conveys all of the world-weary sophistication of an intelligent author-cum-storyteller. But the words cry out for that interpretation. That's how we hear them in our mind when we read them. Not surprising, the images of the film pretty much "show" exactly what is being spoken by the narrator – wonderfully flaunting against the adage of "show don't tell" and "if you are going to tell, don't show exactly what you tell." But Welles, and other filmmakers of that time, paid little heed to that. By hearing, while concurrently being shown the same exact images that are being described, we settle into our being-told-a-story posture. Relax, sit back, and watch/listen. An adult version of "once upon a time..."

Contrast this to the opening of *The Royal Tenenbaums*, in which another voice-of-God narrator, this time performed by Alec Baldwin, never appears in the film.

> NARRATOR (V.O.)
> Royal Tenenbaum bought the house on
> Archer Avenue in the winter of
> his thirty-fifth year.

CUT TO: A five-story limestone townhouse. A forty-three-year-old man in a raincoat rings the front doorbell. He is Royal.

> NARRATOR (CONT'D)
> Over the next decade, he and his wife had
> three children and then they separated.

And then, a little while into the film, the narrator interrupts actual dialogue with:

> NARRATOR (V.O.)
> They were never legally divorced.

We do not yet see his wife or that he had three kids or any visual indication that they are "legally divorced." Does learning this information at this point alter the story? Not really. This information subtly affects the way we process the story, and how we view and feel about the characters. True, we could conceivably learn all of this through normal dialogue exchanges. So why a narrator? What does it give us that learning this same information through regular dialogue couldn't or doesn't give us?

Again, it instantly gives us the magic of storytelling, of being told a story. Sit back and relax ... you are in the hands of a storyteller.

In *500 Days of Summer* the voice-of-God narrator is less a traditional story-teller (even though he says very early on, "This is the story of boy meets girl") than he is an anonymous, opinionated truth-teller. As is often the case, this kind of narrator chimes in at four strategic spots in the narrative demarcating sections of the 114-page script: the beginning (pages 1–3), toward the end of act one (pages 18– 20), at the end of act two (page 85), and at the very end (page 113).

In the beginning, this voice of God tells us something about the mental attitude and belief system of our main character, Tom:

> NARRATOR
> The boy, Tom Hansen of Margate,
> New Jersey, grew up believing that
> he'd never truly be happy until
> the day he met his ... "soulmate."

Could we have learned this another way? Certainly, we could have learned it if Tom was the narrator himself and he just told us this same information in the first person, maybe like this:

> TOM
> My name is Tom Hansen, of Margate,
> New Jersey. I grew up believing that
> I'd never truly be happy until
> the day I met my ... "soulmate."

Is there a difference between the two? Emotionally, do you feel any difference between the two while reading them? I'm not particularly suggesting that one way would be better than the other. I do, however, want to point out that each choice strikes a slightly different emotional chord with an audience. Sometimes, when one speaks about themselves, it can come off as smug, solipsistic, or naïve. Whereas if someone else says the same things about a person, it lets us feel that we're in on something otherwise secret. And in doing so, we might feel slightly more connected to both the character and the narrator since we are now inadvertent co-conspirators with the narrator.

At the very end of *500 Days of Summer*, the voice of God once again chimes in and speculates on what Tom has learned over the course of the entire movie, just as Tom has serendipitously met a potential new girlfriend:

> NARRATOR
> If Tom had learned anything ... it was
> that you can't ascribe great cosmic
> significance to a simple earthly event.

```
Coincidence. That's all anything ever
is. Nothing more than coincidence. It
took a long time but Tom had finally
learned. There are no miracles. There's
no such thing as fate. Nothing is meant
to be. He knew. He was sure of it now.
        (beat)
... pretty sure.
```

Has Tom really learned what the narrator said, or did we, the audience, think this? Or, was it only the thoughts of the narrator? Could the narrator be wrong? That is part of the fun of the voice of God; she can be right, wrong, or both. Whatever the truth is, whether Tom actually consciously now believes that everything was just a coincidence, us hearing it from the voice-of-God narrator engages us in collaborating with this voice as we, too, muse over whether love is coincidence or fate. Of course, this is heard as we see that Tom will clearly have a romantic shot with a new person that he has just met. We leave the film feeling good for Tom and in a way feeling that we know a bit more about him than even he knows about himself. This is the power of the omniscient voice-of-God-type of narration.

Looking-back V.O.

The voice of a character that reminisces about a time in her past but is either not at all seen in the narrative or seen only peripherally to the main story.

The looking-back V.O. is sometimes a pure reminiscence. It immediately conjures an air of nostalgia, oftentimes tinged with melancholy. There are two kinds of looking-back V.O.s: either a character from within the story is looking back and has minimal screen time as their older self, or a character speaks to us from the future that we never see at the age that they are speaking from.

A great example of the former – a voice-over from a character that is looking back at a time in his life decades ago but has minimal screen time – is, again, *Stand by Me*. In the movie adapted from a Stephen King novella, *The Body*, the actor Richard Dreyfuss plays an adult character named Gordon who recalls an episode of his youth. In this particular example, the film begins with us actually seeing the adult Gordon sitting in his Land Rover while pensively peering out his windshield, remembering:

```
                NARRATOR
        (Adult Gordon)
I was twelve going on thirteen the first
time I saw a dead human being. It
happened in the summer of
nineteen-fifty-nine. A long time ago.
```

> But only if you measure in terms of
> years. I was living in a small town
> in Oregon called Castle Rock. There
> were only 1281 people, but to me
> it was the whole world.

Nostalgia, melancholy, and self-reflection. The tone is set. And if you are astute enough to remember the headline of the newspaper lying open on his dashboard, you might recall that it says, "Local attorney fatally stabbed in restaurant." But since it's the very beginning of the film, with the theme music swelling with a visual of "GORDON LACHANCE, 37" sitting in his car amidst a country road deep in thought, all you might have absorbed was Gordon's voice-over narration – and that would have been enough to set the tone: nostalgia, melancholy, and self-reflection.

We see Gordon as an adult for less than a minute before a seamless dissolve brings us back to where he is remembering, just as we hear his narration say, "It happened in the summer or nineteen-fifty-nine." This is a perfect usage of a looking-back V.O. where the narrator is looking back and is also seen – though very briefly. His narration, the words that he's saying and why he's saying them, are justified by the end of the film. In other words, the narration is not an arbitrary commenting on a story, but rather, is actually the words of an article that adult Gordon is writing. The film is about twelve-year-old Gordon, "Gordie"; his best friends Chris, Teddy, and Vern; and their overnight journey to see a dead body. The characters, especially young Gordon, go through a coming-of-age character arc, and in a way so does the adult Gordon go through his own minor arc.

As was previously discussed, when we first meet the boys in their treehouse, we hear adult Gordon's voice-over describe that "Chris was the leader of our gang, and my best friend." It is interesting that in this case, much of what we hear in voice-over can actually be seen, which if not clear here, will soon be self-evident. Nevertheless, telling us early on that Chris came from a bad family and that he has a complex about it is information that we can't immediately see. It's true that much later on in the story, Chris admits a version of the complexity of his relationship to his family and how he's perceived by the community. But at this early part of our story, for us to be told this information, even though we don't see him being "bad," widens our sympathy and empathy toward him. This is a good usage of voice-over, giving us information that we can't see which helps us get closer to our characters.

This idea of giving us insight into characters through voice-overs can go even further when, not unlike the third person author of a novel, the voice-over also gives us insight about life in general. A wonderful example of this occurs just after the midpoint of the film when the four boys are lounging around a campfire, basking in the afterglow of an enchantingly wonderfully gross story that young Gordon (Gordie) has just told them all. As they chat away with a fleeting innocence and earnestness, we hear the narrator, adult Gordon, say:

> NARRATOR (V.O.)
> We talked into the night. The
> kind of talk that seemed important,
> until you discover girls.

In juxtaposition to what we then hear young Gordon say to his friends:

> GORDON
> Alright, alright, Mickey's a
> mouse. Donald's a duck. Pluto's
> a dog. What's Goofy?

Of course, we can *see* them "talking into the night," but the added commentary about this moment through voice-over rings true to our ears and sensibilities, especially as we then see and hear the narrator's younger self earnestly question the identity of a Disney cartoon creature. He is clearly among the last spasms of pre-adolescent innocence and worries that he'll never have it again. And we, too, revel in the wonderfully mindless and mythically sublime innocence that we once had before we discovered …

At the very end of the film, we see adult Gordon finish typing as we hear his final thoughts about the entire story that we had just seen, and that he had been writing about:

> NARRATOR (V.O.)
> I never had any friends later on
> like the ones I had when I was
> twelve. Jesus, does anyone?

And with that, the adult Gordon leaves his typewriter to be with his own twelve-year-old son while the theme music of the song *Stand by Me* rises and the film fades out to a satisfying end. We see adult Gordon on screen at the end for less than two minutes, barely three minutes of total screen time, but it is essential to our whole experience. We have heard him, his musings, his deepest thoughts as a wizened voice-over narration in the beginning, and only a few more times for brief comments, observations, and insights. Could this story be told without ever seeing him on screen at all and just seeing the kids? Possibly. But the bigger question might be: could this story be told and still have created its soulful, longing tone without his voice-over narration at all? I don't think so.

This is a terrific example of looking-back voice-over when the voice of that character still has a minimal, nearly peripheral role, within the whole of the narrative. And it's integral in creating a satisfying tone. A big reason for this is that just as young Gordon completes his character arc of his own coming-of-age, leaving his boyhood and entering "manhood" as an acknowledged storyteller, confronting the death of his brother, and ultimately taking a stand to defend his best friend Chris, adult Gordon also completes his own minor character arc. True, adult Gordon's arc is not nearly as dramatic as his younger self, but it is oddly satisfying to the audience. Adult Gordon voices his own epiphany about youth and the ineffable sacred bond of youthful friendships that can never again be replicated. In doing so, this adds an extra dimension of completeness to both Gordons, young and adult.

We can speculate on how *we* might write this film without any voice-over narration. Perhaps we would create two parallel stories so that what is heard through voice-over might be expressed in actual scenes, with adult Gordon speaking to other characters we'd have to create. We'd also have to create situations that would allow both Gordons to voice similar thoughts as we learned through the voice-over. The film *Stand by Me* is barely ninety minutes long. To keep the story of the boys and create another one for adult Gordon would add significant time to it. As is, it is a short feature film, a perfect soufflé of a full experience. Voice-over narration with a character we actually see years later helps to make that happen.

There are many examples of looking-back voice-overs in which the person whose voice we hear is seen, but only peripherally, like in *Stand by Me*. Among these films and TV shows are *The Princess Bride*, *The Life of Pi*, *Citizen Kane*, and *The Big Lebowski*. In *Lebowski*, The Stranger/narrator is barely seen a few times as a passing commentator, only a corporeal voice-of-God who somehow adds just enough lunacy through his presence that it helps us enjoy the lunacy of the crazy tale being told. In *Citizen Kane*, the narrator is a curious reporter trying to solve the psychological mystery of an enigmatic man, only to learn that some mysteries of the mind will never be understood.

In both *The Princess Bride* and *The Life of Pi*, just as in *Stand by Me*, the narrators have lesser stories, but each still has a mini character arc or epiphany of their own that contributes tremendously to the satisfaction level that these films engender. In each of these particular films, the entire notion of story and mythology is prominent among their themes. All the more fitting, then, to *have a voice-over storyteller help to weave the magic web of suspending our disbelief.*

* * *

Examples of the looking-back voice-over in which we never actually see the character at the age or time that we hear them speaking are fewer. But one of the great ones is *To Kill a Mockingbird*. It is interesting to deconstruct *Mockingbird's* voice-over since, similar to *Stand by Me*, *500 Days of Summer*, and numerous others, the voice-overs appear strategic, marking structural points in the timing of the narrative. The placement of a voice-over can illustrate a logical positioning and function of when and where to have a narrator speak to us, while leading the audience toward concerns and themes that the screenwriter (and her character) finds essential. Like in *Stand by Me,* the voice-over in *Mockingbird* is also from the older self of a character that the film is concerned with. In this case, the young girl that we focus on is nicknamed Scout and her voice-over name is Jean Louise, her real name. We never see the adult version of Scout in the film, but it doesn't matter. This narrator is simply content in telling us her personal life tale.

To Kill a Mockingbird was a hugely popular Pulitzer Prize–winning novel by Harper Lee. It subsequently became a multiple Academy Award–winning film in 1962. Adapted by the accomplished playwright Horton Foote, it deals with big themes, including racism, intellectual disability, dignity, and heroism. The novel was written from Jean Louise's first-person point-of-view and the film maintains this perspective by way of her first-person voice-over narration. The original film script was 146 pages, which is considered long by today's standards of scriptwriting and doesn't precisely meet the generally accepted sense that one page equals one minute of screen time as the film was 129 minutes long. It is interesting to note that percentagewise, the placement of the voice-over in both the script and the film is relatively the same: there is a voice-over in the beginning, at the midpoint, at the beginning of act three, and at the very end. The first one sets up the tone and suggests that something of great import will happen:

> JEAN LOUISE'S VOICE
> In 1932 this was the world I knew.
> It wasn't a very big world, but neither
> was I. (a beat) I was six years old.

THE CAMERA STARTS TO SLOWLY MOVE DOWN the main residential street leading away from the Square.

> JEAN LOUISE'S VOICE
> They tell me Maycomb was a tired old
> town then, that people moved slowly.
> There was no hurry for there was
> nowhere to go, nothing to buy and no
> money to buy it with.

During this THE CAMERA HAS COME TO REST ON the Finch house and yard. The Finch house is a small frame house, built high off the ground and with a porch in the manner of Southern cottages of its day. The yard is a large one, filled with oaks, and it all has an air of mystery about it in the early morning light.

> JEAN LOUISE'S VOICE
> What I remember was that I was to begin
> school in two weeks, for the first time.
> What I didn't know was that my whole
> world was soon to change.

The second voice-over comes exactly in the middle of the film and the screenplay. It comes just as Scout and her brother Jem stare "wide-eyed" at the contents of Jem's cigar box: fascinating objects from their mysterious and intellectually challenged neighbor, Boo Radley. Horton Foote elected not to place a voice-over at the end of act one, but it is interesting that the first two structural points, the end of act one and the midpoint, are both concerned with the kids' budding connection and fascination with Boo Radley. Of course, by the midpoint we also know that their father, Atticus Finch, is defending Tom, a local African-American man falsely accused of rape. But of primary importance to the story is how Atticus stands up against the entire white population of the town and how his children are also ostracized and affected by their father's stand and integrity.

CLOSE SHOT - SCOUT She is looking at the watch. She is google-eyed. Jem holds the soap figures of the boy and girl he found in the knothole. CAMERA PULLS INTO CLOSE SHOT of the TWO SOAP FIGURES.

>   JEAN LOUISE'S VOICE
>   It was to be a long time before Jem
>   and I talked about Boo again.

DISSOLVE TO:

INT. RADLEY HOUSE Early in February. Scout and Jem come by. They are using sticks as guns.

>   JEAN LOUISE'S VOICE
>   Christmas came and was gone. Jem had a
>   birthday. Otherwise, the time was quiet
>   and uneventful until one day early in
>   February. Jem and I decided to go hunting.

Other than telling us that time has moved forward and that life has continued on, there is not much, if any, important information. There is no particular insight, description, or information regarding what Scout is thinking. So why is the voice-over placed here? And what does it have to do with the notion of "pushing the story forward"? The answer is that it doesn't. What it does do, however, is remind us that an older Scout, Jean Louise, is telling us this story and that she has reentered in voice-over at moments of mystery and magic, like when Scout stares "google-eyed" at the objects inside her brother's cigar box at what is essentially the unique mind of Boo Radley. It is an oddly emotional choice that earmarks the placement of this voice-over. But now we are fully bonded with the kids' connection to Boo Radley and the story is able to shift seamlessly into the second half of the narrative that focuses almost entirely on the extreme racism of the town, the trial of Tom, and his subsequent murder. After all this has transpired midway through act three with more story still to tell, we hear adult Scout's voice-over that simply marks some distance in time since Tom's death. Again, it refers to her Boo Radley fascination, not the racial strife that we have been watching, which keeps us consistently connected to her wistful curiosity about things like the alienation of outsiders and the disenfranchised.

CLOSE SHOT The knothole of the oak is front of the
Radley house. The trunk is swelling around the cement
patch. The patch itself is turning yellow. Leaves fall
from the branches of the tree. CAMERA PULLS BACK as WE
SEE the Radley house and sidewalk.

> JEAN LOUISE'S VOICE
> By October things had settled down again. I
> still looked for Boo every time I went
> by the Radley place. Maybe some day I would
> still see him. I imagined how it would be when
> it happened. He'd just be setting on the swing
> when I came along, "Hidy do, Mr. Arthur," I
> would say as if I had said it every afternoon
> of
> my life. "Evenin', Jean Louise," he would say as
> if he had said it every afternoon of my life.
> "Right pretty spell we're having, isn't it?"
> "Yes, sir, right pretty" I would say and go on.

Aside from telling us that time has passed and that Scout is still fascinated by the mysterious neighbor that she could only imagine, it also sets up the thrilling conclusion of the story:

Scout and Jem walk past Radley's house towards school.
Jem has her by the hand and in the other, he is
carrying a costume that Scout is to wear in a pageant
that evening.

> JEAN LOUISE'S VOICE
> This night my mind was filled with Halloween.
> There was to be a pageant representing
> our country's agricultural products. I was
> to be a Ham. My duties, as I gathered from
> our two rehearsals, were to come on stage
> left when Miss Stephanie call "Pork." Jem
> said he would escort me to the school
> auditorium. Thus began our longest journey
> together.

We are now set up for our conclusion and resolution. After Boo Radley saves the life of Scout's badly injured brother and it's clear that Jem will live and the assailant will not, Jean Louise sums it all up for us at the very end:

```
EXT. FINCH FRONT PORCH AND SIDEWALK - MOVING SHOT -
NIGHT
They walk in the yard, up the walk and onto the Radley
porch. Arthur finds the door knob and goes in, leaving
Scout alone on the porch.

                    JEAN LOUISE (V.O.)
          Neighbors bring food with death, and
          flowers with sickness, and little things
          in between. Boo was our neighbor. He gave
          us two soap dolls, a broken watch and chain,
          a knife and our lives. One time Atticus
          said you never really knew a man until you
          stood in his shoes and walked around in them.
          Just standing on the Radley porch was enough.


MOVING SHOT
Scout starts home. A fine rain is falling. She runs up
the steps and goes into her house.

DISSOLVE TO:

INT. JEM'S BEDROOM

Atticus is there, sitting beside Jem's bed.

                    SCOUT
          Has Jem waked up yet?

                    ATTICUS
          Sleeping peacefully. He won't wake
          until morning.

She climbs into his lap.

                    JEAN LOUISE (V.O.)
          Well, the summer that had begun so
          long ago had ended, and another summer
          had taken its place, and a fall, and Boo
```

```
                 Radley had come out and Jem was to live.
                 I was to think of these days many times,
                 of Jem, and Dill and Boo Radley and Tom
                 Robinson and the Ewells and Atticus -- his
                 fairness, his stubbornness, his devotion,
                 his courage, his love.


EXT. FINCH HOUSE - JEM'S WINDOW
We can SEE Atticus through the window, sitting by his
son's bed, holding Scout.

                                  JEAN LOUISE (V.O.)
                 He would be in Jem's room all night
                 and he would be there when Jem waked up
                 in the morning.


CAMERA SLOWLY PULLS BACK as Atticus looks at the
sleeping Jem.
FADE OUT
```

And with that, the film fades out to the end. We are left with a portrait of a uniquely heroic family, who are very humane, though nearly mundanely relatable. We have just lived through enormous racial strife, injustice, and tragedy. We have also lived through tremendous love and courageousness, the mystery and curiosity of a child's mind, and the ways in which it processes challenging life events. The voice-over throughout never speaks about racial themes or about Boo's disabilities. It constantly grounds us in the prosaicness of living, of the courage to face tomorrow. Once again, the voice-over eludes some common misconceptions. Sometimes it barely has to move the narrative forward or give us insight into the minds of the characters to be effective. Sometimes, like in *To Kill a Mockingbird*, it can even help elucidate the ineffable.

Part-of-the-narrative V.O.

When a character sometimes speaks in voice-over but is also an active part of the on-screen narrative.

A few prominent examples of "Part-of-the-narrative V.O.": *Memento, The Shawshank Redemption, The Usual Suspects, The Princess Bride, Badlands, Taxi Driver, Trainspotting.*

There are numerous variations of part-of-the-narrative V.O. For example, we might hear a voice-over narration from a character that we're watching on screen and *eventually* learn that the narration is from a future scene. When we finally get to that scene, we realize that the narration that we've been hearing is actually dialogue that our character is speaking to a psychiatrist or judge, a story being told to their child at bedtime, or a thought being spoken aloud or written in their diary. Upon learning the source and reason for what had been narration, we are suddenly able to stitch together everything that we've seen and learned up to that point in an extra-satisfying understanding of the narrative. Mindy Kaling does a great job of illustrating this in her TV pilot *The Mindy Project*. (NOTE: In this early drafts she's called "Mira," but subsequently changed to "Mindy.") At the top of the cold open, we see her speaking directly to us "in smudged makeup and a crumpled cocktail dress":

> MIRA
> You have an idea of how your life is
> going to work out. When I was a kid,
> all I did was watch romantic comedies
> in our living room while I did my
> homework.

But for the next four pages, we watch Mira go through a series of scenes as we continue to hear her in voice-over narration. The scenes have real-time dialogue in them, as well as Mira's V.O. narrations commenting on what we're watching. We believe that she's speaking directly to us, the audience.

> MIRA (V.O.)
> In college, I had less time to watch
> Movies ... And then, eventually, I had
> no time at all ...

But at the bottom of page four, we see that Mira has been actually talking to a female police officer in a police station all along. Now we are more enticed than ever; why is she speaking with smudged makeup to a policewoman? When the narrative returns back to the various scenes leading up to this moment we now know who she's speaking to, and we are even more compelled to watch and find out exactly how and why she ended up at a police station. Watching Mira at the wedding of her ex-boyfriend, we hear her tell the policewoman:

> MIRA (V.O.)
> He dumped me, she moved in, he fixed
> her teeth. They got married last night.
> I don't think they thought I would actually
> go, so they invited me. But I did go.

Eventually, by the end of the cold open with Mira's V.O. now making complete and endearingly pathetic sense, we watch her get completely sloshed, make a royal mess at the wedding, and end up nearly drowning. Thus, the V.O. thoroughly explains why she's at the police station, bonding us with her character and compelling us to want to continue watching.

Just as Mira speaks only a minimal amount of voice-over and is still an essential part of the story going forward, there are numerous other examples where V.O. is employed to a greater extent. Case in point: Verbal Kint, played by Kevin Spacey in *The Usual Suspects*, is both actively involved as a character on screen and off screen throughout the entire film. As Verbal is being interrogated by the police, we hear in V.O. the story he tells them. By hearing his words, his character becomes unusually reliable, lulling us into believing him. We take him at his word all the way until the shocking ending when his true character is revealed.

On occasion, a running narration by a character that's an integral part of the narrative is just that: someone narrating, telling us the story we're watching as we watch it. *Trainspotting* is a fantastic example of this. The narrator, Renton, comments in V.O. all throughout the film. But his language is always authentic, wry, funny, ironic, and full of argot, which makes us feel more privy to his world. Here's Renton, setting up the theme and tone of the story:

```
                 RENTON (V.O.)
People think it's all about misery and
desperation and death and all that shite,
which is not to be ignored, but what they
forget - Spud is shooting up for the
pleasure of it. Otherwise we wouldn't do
it. After all, we're not fucking stupid.
At least, we're not that fucking stupid.
Take the best orgasm you ever had, multiply
it by a thousand and you're still nowhere
near it. When you're on junk you have only
one worry: scoring. When you're off it you
are suddenly obliged to worry about all sorts
of other shite. Got no money: can't get
pished. Got money: drinking too much. Can't
get a bird: no chance of a ride. Got a bird:
too much hassle. You have to worry about
bills, about food, about some football team
that never fucking wins, about human
relationships and all the things that really
don't matter when you've got a sincere and
truthful junk habit.
```

In the case of *The Usual Suspects*, Verbal's V.O. is essential toward creating the powerful and surprising ending. It helps to misdirect our trust. Hearing a voice-over narrator is often soothing ... and trusting. In *The Shawshank Redemption*, Red's V.O. throughout, as well as his presence on screen, deepens our trust in him and his perception. In this case, his voice-over, full of wry bits of wisdom, goes a long way toward making this film so beloved and satisfying.

>   RED (V.O.)
>   There's a con like me in every prison
>   in America, I guess. I'm the guy who can
>   get it for you. Cigarettes, a bag of reefer
>   if you're partial, a bottle of brandy to
>   celebrate your kid's high school graduation.
>   Damn near anything, within reason.

He slips somebody a pack of smokes, a smooth sleight-of-hand.

>   RED (V.O.)
>   Yes sir, I'm a regular Sears & Roebuck.

TWO SHORT SIREN BLASTS issue from the main tower, drawing everybody's attention to the loading dock. The outer gate swings open ... revealing a gray prison bus outside.

>   RED (V.O.)
>   So when Andy Dufresne came to me in 1949 and
>   asked me to smuggle Rita Hayworth into the
>   prison for him, I told him no problem. And
>   it wasn't.

Red is both a wonderful storyteller and a sympathetic guide. His voice-over narration helps, in a significant way, to create and sustain the film's beloved and compassionate tone.

When is it appropriate to use voice-overs?

Not every story calls for using voice-over. But there is no set rule, no specific metric that determines whether to use this technique. Yes, it can bring a cozy tone. Yes, it can add an extra dimension or layer of insight or depth. But it isn't required.

A few things to keep in mind when considering whether to use V.O.:

- Is your story a remembrance?
- Does a character need to tell us information beyond what can be seen and heard in real time?
- Is your character's voice worthy of being heard beyond her normal dialogue?

- Would a narration help establish a specific tone?
- Does a character need to have her "voice" and personality expressed beyond her real-time interactions within the narrative?
- Are you deliberately trying to create distance and/or perspective between your story and your audience?
- Does your story require additional context?
- Are you consciously attempting to call attention to your story's mythic nature?
- Are you trying to add a meta-layer?
- Are you attempting to create a literary dimension?
- Do you need to lull the audience into added trust?
- Would you like to create an obvious story-listener–story-teller relationship?
- Are you striving for a "cozy" once-upon-a-time tone?
- Do you want us to hear the voice of a deceased person (or set up the notion of an afterlife or spiritual universe?)
- Would you like to establish an inner life of a character that is considerably different from what is being portrayed by her actions and dialogue on screen?

At the end of the day, deciding whether to use voice-over is a personal decision. What are the films and TV shows that you love that have V.O.? Does your story lend itself to *feeling* like other screen narratives that use voice-over?

5

PLATFORMS

Introduction: Platforms

Scripted "speaking," the memorializing of conversation, monologues to and with others, speaking to oneself aloud, or in one's mind, began as the verbal component within religious ritual. Either through word-of-mouth or notation, words were often committed to memory and intoned upon various auspicious and sacred occasions. Eventually, prepared texts intended to be spoken aloud found expression in theatrical dramas and prose within which descriptions of what people said was called for. Ultimately, it evolved to include film and television as well. For the purposes of this book, I consider video games and other new-media platforms as extensions of the film and TV entertainment experience and thus, dialogue-wise, they adhere to the same rules, conditions, and demands.

Are there really differences in dialogue writing between the various platforms most common to scripted dialogue: film, TV, theater, and prose? The answer has never been less clear. And that, as far as I'm concerned, is good news. In the current narrative-making environment, anything goes. New hybrids and mash-ups are constantly evolving, popping up in every aspect of scripted narratives and borrowing from various platforms can seamlessly add a certain meta-dimension to a story. I'm not specifically referring to mixing genres or styles (drama and comedy equal *dramedy*) or even tonal juxtaposition (combining violence and humor). However, sometimes new forms rely on grabbing elements from various platforms and shaking them up; a couple of examples are episodic musical shows, like *Crazy Ex-Girlfriend* (2015), as well as hyper-stylized theatrical techniques in film, like *Ferris Bueller's Day Off* (1986) or *Natural Born Killers* (1994). It is with this idea of possible hybrid combinations that it is beneficial to be familiar with the basic dialogue platforms, their usages, and what they're known for. The following, then, is a cursory review of the traditional kinds of dialogue that are common to the equally traditional platforms they are associated with.

Theater

In many respects, theater is primarily an oral and aural form more than it is a visual medium. There are many great plays in which you can literally close your eyes, only listen to the production and still thoroughly attain the intended theatrical experience. This is achieved not just by listening to expertly delivered dialogue, but also through hearing the entire aural soundscape of the production: the exaggerated clomping of obviously artificial horse hooves, the purposeful clinging of sabers in faux combat, and the unique sound of live music emanating from the stage. The live theater experience is far less dependent on visuals, even though fantastic sets, imaginative staging, and the actors' visual presence can raise the experience to an even higher level. One of my greatest early theatrical experiences was listening to a recording of a Royal Shakespeare production of *Othello* with headphones. All of the pomp and theatricality of the production leapt alive in my mind's eye, simply from hearing it.

The entire stage experience is unabashedly make-believe; sounds, visuals, gestures, and languages are commonly exaggerated, *representational,* and artistically artificial. These are the hallmarks of theater and are what audiences desire from a live theatrical experience. Live theater demands a suspension of disbelief far greater than in film and television. And as theatergoers, we are mostly willing to suspend our propensity for reality.

To experience a play, we attend a specific space that houses a specific stage with a set that is clearly not the actual location of the play itself. In *Hamlet*, the set is on a stage, not truly in Denmark. Similarly, the actor we watch is a living person who is acting on that stage, pretending that he is a king when we clearly know that when the play is over, he too will go home, just like we will. This *pretending,* so common for children, is what live theater trades and depends on. When you go to a play, you are agreeing to be a collaborator within illusion and *make-believe.* When a child holds up a toy action figure, moves it around, and speaks for it, she doesn't use her natural voice. She automatically speaks in her version of her character. When she strains to alter her voice, anyone hearing her knows it's her altered voice. Similarly, dialogue for plays is often equally exaggerated, catering to the collective magic that the production attempts to conjure. In theater, characters often represent their greater symbolic archetypes; they exist nearly as avatars.

Euripides, Sophocles, and Aeschylus are considered the greatest of the ancient Greek tragedians. Their plays have deeply influenced what we consider our Western theatrical tradition. It is not too difficult to imagine that their words, dialogue, and themes arose directly from sacred Dionysian rites that used song and verbal incantations within their ceremonies. In this way, these dramatists preserved and instilled their cultural values and ethos. Their use of soliloquies and asides (covered in Chapter Three) in which characters speak directly to the audience, became a mainstay device for future theater. Here are three, of many, famous quotes from Euripides's tragedies – *Medea, Orestes,* and *Alcestis* – that speak to the resounding wisdom of his dialogue.

> When love is in excess it brings a man no honor nor worthiness.

> One loyal friend is worth ten thousand relatives.

> When a good man is hurt, all who would be called good must suffer with him.

It is important to remember that these words are spoken by characters to other characters, or directly to the audience as dialogue within plays. Even if they are representational of archetypal men and women, they are obviously far from natural sounding, realistic conversation. Their language is much more oratorical and pontifical than normal conversation, and thus are thoroughly stage-worthy and able to fill the grandness of their themes within a large theatrical setting. Suddenly, a playwright could use a character to voice a range of subjects, often polemical in nature, in heightened and eloquent ways, and outside of the pulpit of religion.

Over a millennium later, it's nearly impossible to think of theater dialogue without William Shakespeare coming to mind. And yet, his debt to ancient Greek drama is ever-present. The voices of his characters, whether through the legions of his memorable quotes or his witty repartee, remain resonate and nearly modern-sounding today.

Let's look at a snippet of a scene from Shakespeare's wonderfully theatrical *All's Well That Ends Well,* in which Bertram attempts to woo Diana. Notice how it resembles actual conversation while living in a heightened make-believe universe.

Enter BERTRAM and the maid called DIANA.

BERTRAM
They told me that your name was Fontybell.

DIANA
No, my good lord, Diana.

> BERTRAM
>
> Titled goddess;
> And worth it, with addition! But, fair soul,
> In your fine frame hath love no quality?
> If quick fire of youth light not your mind
> You are no maiden, but a monument.
> When you are dead, you should be such a one
> As you are now; for you are cold and stem,
> And now you should be as your mother was
> When your sweet self was got.
>
> DIANA
>
> She then was honest.
>
> BERTRAM
>
> So should you be.
>
> DIANA
>
> No.
> My mother did but duty; such, my lord,
> As you owe to your wife.
>
> BERTRAM
>
> No more a' that!
> I prithee do not strive against my vows;
> I was compell'd to her, but I love thee
> By love's own sweet constraint, and will for ever
> Do thee all rights of service.
>
> DIANA
>
> Ay, so you serve us
> Till we serve you; but when you have our roses,
> You barely leave our thorns to prick ourselves,
> And mock us with our bareness.
>
> BERTRAM
>
> How have I sworn!

Yes, it's anachronistic, stylized, and certainly not the way that people today talk, but it is also smart, wise, and entertaining. It is also complex and suggests that Diana has her own intentions in store for Bertram, thus moving the intricate gears of the story along. In many respects, when we think of dialogue in plays, we expect it *not* to be the way that we actually speak. It would be disappointing if it were so ordinary. We expect theater dialogue to be extraordinary, thoughtful, witty, and more full of wisdom than ordinary conversation. Theater dialogue has been heightened and nonrealistic since its origins.

Exaggerated dialogue can and does definitely find its way into modern film and television. The key to our accepting it is in cajoling the audience into collaborating in the make-believeness of the event. Remember, we nearly expect it in a live theatrical setting. However, cuing the audience of a film or television show into being predisposed to equally accepting it is the real challenge. One way to do this is to visually proclaim that what we are seeing is not meant to be realistic. In *The Wizard of Oz* (1939), once we are in the ultra-stylized universe of Oz, characters can speak equally as stylized and heightened as in theater:

```
              PROFESSOR
That's right. Here -- sit right down here.
That's it. Ha ha! This -- this is the same
genuine, magic, authentic crystal used by
the Priests of Isis and Osiris in the days of
the Pharaohs of Egypt -- in which Cleopatra
first saw the approach of Julius Caesar and
Marc Anthony, and -- and so on -- and so on.
Now, you -- you'd better close your eyes, my
child, for a moment -- in order to be better
in tune with the infinite. We -- we can't do
these things without ... reaching out into
the infinite.
```

Another way to draw a film or television audience into a world that allows unrealistic dialogue is to simply establish the heightened tone from the very beginning, as we saw in Chapter Three with *Moonstruck* (1987). The point is, heightened and exaggerated dialogue can work in film and television if it's contextualized within the style of the greater piece, or proclaimed right away as a conceit of the style. This kind of *theatrical* dialogue has been an integral part of dramatic writing since the very beginning.

Film

With flickering lights and a luminescent glow, *film* brought the realism of photographs into contiguous motion pictures. Whereas from a seat in the back half of the audience of a live play it is virtually impossible to read the sudden nuanced downturn of a character's mouth on stage, in film, by way of a close-up, that same character's expression is clearly seen and understood. In a play, you wouldn't write a stage direction in the script like: *She overhears their conversation and seems somewhat distressed.* This is mostly because you simply couldn't direct the live audience's attention to the "she" that you're describing. But screenwriters do this all the time in a screenplay. (The example I just cited was from the original *Star Wars*, 1977.)

While in theater we are asked to make-believe that an actor on a stage is a king, in film, we can not only view the pores of his skin, but also witness in realistic detail his *actual* castle. *Within this process of visual and aural intimacy and accuracy, the business of audience collaboration in believing the efficacy of the ongoing artifice is made all the more easy and palatable.* While in plays, characters are more *representative* of their symbolic prototype-selves, in film, they are assumed to be the actual embodiment of their real character-selves. Consequently, we assume that their dialogue in films hews toward being equally authentic. And in film, "authentic" can also describe pedestrian, quotidian, or human behavior. Because of the absolutely realistic settings in film, characters have a greater opportunity to react to those settings in much the same way that the viewer would in the real world. This can serve to further bond an audience with film characters; they act, react, and *speak* just like us, or at least more closely to the way that we want to speak.

This sheds light on why films about other eras, both past and future, as well as those fantastical in nature, tend to bring commonplace or modernesque attitudes, including fun, prosaic dialogue, into their otherwise reality-specific universes. Take the opening of *Iron Man* (2008) as an example:

```
INT. HUMMER - CONTINUOUS

Three Airmen, kids with battle-worn faces. Crammed in
there with them is a Man in an expensive suit, who
looks teleported from Beverly Hills. He is, of course,
genius inventor and billionaire, TONY STARK. In his
hand is a drink tumbler of vodka.

                    TONY
          Oh, I get it. You guys aren't allowed
          to talk. Is that it? Are you not
          allowed to talk?

One Airman grins, fidgeting with his orange NY Mets
watch.

                    JIMMY
          No. We're allowed to talk.

                    TONY
          Oh. I see. So it's personal.

                    RAMIREZ
          I think they're intimidated.
```

```
                    TONY
       Good God, you're a woman.

The others try to compress laughs.
                 TONY (CONT'D)
       I, honestly, I couldn't have called
       that.
            (after silence)
       I would apologize, but isn't that
       what we're going for here? I saw you
       as a soldier first.

                    JIMMY
       I have a question, sir.

                    TONY
       Please.
```

The Marvel Universe is certainly unrealistic and yet, almost by contrast, the dialogue is extremely contemporary and nearly mundane as it reveals who Tony, the human, is.

We don't have to spend too much time considering how the platform of film dictates specific dialogue, because it doesn't. Film dialogue, as we've discussed, can be as varied as can be imagined. But generally, it skews toward being realistic, or as realistic as the tone of the overall project suggests. The film *Clueless* (1995) is set within a realistic Beverly Hills neighborhood, but includes exaggerated dialogue and an exaggeratedly comical plot. These elements allow us to not only seamlessly accept the exaggerations, but also to thoroughly enjoy them. Comedy allows for greater latitude in tones of dialogue, since by its very nature, the situations themselves are often exaggerated. Dove-tailing the overall tone of the production with the tone of the dialogue is the most important factor to consider.

TV

In many respects, television, productions intended to be viewed on smaller screens other than in movie theaters, has become a unique blend of film and theater. It is not as exaggerated or representational as theater, and not as filmic and visually reliant as film. Instead, the television medium has found a hybrid sweet spot between the two. If theater tends to rely on dialogue more than film, then television also is dialogue heavy in lieu of purely visual storytelling.

One major signifier of traditional television writing is that *character* dominates the logic and appeal of successful shows. Audiences fall in love with characters and want to return to them again and again. It is the consistency of character, their unique appeal, the way their minds work, and their predictability that draws us into feeling comfortable with them. Their dialogue, including the cadence of how they speak, is as much a component of why we like to watch them as the way that they look.

But the definition of what constitutes a purely television experience today is totally without limits. Digital platforms such as Netflix and Amazon, to name but a few of them, have helped to push any previous definition of what constitutes television content into brand new configurations. If a traditional-length "film" is made by Netflix and is consumed on a computer screen or television set, should we consider it a film or a TV show? (I'd view it as a film to be watched on TV!) As recently as a decade ago, half-hour television content was exclusive to comedies, whereas one-hour content was exclusive to dramas. Though today those definitions remain somewhat true in network programming, they are quickly being morphed into various new hybrids. Half-hour shows such as *Girls* (2012) or *Louie* (2010) defy being categorized as purely comedic and they are certainly not traditional sitcoms.

Sitcom writing, that is the writing for *situational comedies,* is nearly a separate category of script writing unto itself. Part joke-telling, part character-driven story, the traditional sitcom form has had rigorous rules and demands built into the thirty-minute structure: very limited page-count; around three or four commercial breaks; an A, B, C plot; and a certain amount of setups and laugh-punches per page. The following is a prime example of sitcom writing from an episode of *Two and a Half Men* (2003):

```
CHARLIE, ALAN AND JAKE ARE EATING CHINESE TAKE-OUT.
JAKE HAS A CASE OF SNIFFLES. USING CHOPSTICKS, CHARLIE
TAKES A PIECE OF FOOD OUT OF A TAKE-OUT BOX AND HOLDS
IT UP FOR JAKE TO EAT.

                    CHARLIE
          Here, try this.

                     JAKE
          - What is it? -
                    CHARLIE
          Just try it.

                     JAKE
          Hey, that's good.

                    CHARLIE
          Of course it is. It's chicken in
          frumunda sauce.

                     JAKE
          Frumunda sauce?
```

                        CHARLIE
        Yeah, from unda' the toilet.

                        JAKE
        Get it, Dad?

                        ALAN
        Yeah, I get it. I got it 30 years
        ago, the first time he said it.

                        CHARLIE
        Yeah, but it's new to him. ... Check
        this out. Hey, Jake? What do you call
        the red mushy stuff between the
        elephant's toes? -

                        JAKE
        What?

                        CHARLIE
        ... Slow-moving natives. ... I love
        this kid. He's a comedy blank slate.

                        ALAN
        I'm glad you do, but you might not
        want to share your chopsticks with
        him. ... I think he's coming down with
        something.

                        CHARLIE
        - Oh, no. He thinks it's a head cold
        but it's snot.

This is page one of this episode. Not only is it full of jokes, but it also sets up the eventual "cold" that Alan gets, which is an integral part of the A plot that is set in motion by Charlie a few moments later in this same scene. Sitcom writing is fast-paced and witty while managing to move multiple storylines forward. And the key to sitcom storylines is that they are typically directly connected to the various idiosyncrasies of the core characters in the show. Thus, in *Two and a Half Men*, Charlie is consistently successful, crude, and sex-obsessed while his brother, Alan, is always sincere and a loser. And their dialogue always stays true to their character traits.

Especially in unique hybrids, the mixture of character, story, and theatricality take on whole new television categories. *Fleabag* (2016) is a prime example of this. As much tragicomedy as comedy and with episodes less than a half-hour, it manages to transform the purely theatrical devices of its staged source material into something wholly unique. Relying on a wall of manic, deeply honest, and self-deprecatory dialogue, *Fleabag* is a great model for the potential of new and exciting television to come.

In one-hour television episodes, which are traditionally dramatic in nature, character traits equally dominate the appeal of successful shows. However, with an entire hour to fill, plot and narrative become more important than relying on one-liners. Nevertheless, dialogue-heavy shows, such as *The West Wing* (1999), manage to have complex stories, as well as nonstop, high-level word play. Whereas traditional police or medical *procedurals* tend to be more plot-driven and less dialogue-dependent, there are certainly wonderful exceptions to this, such as *House* (2004) and *True Detective* (2014). Both feature complex, verbose dialogue that is innate to specific characters, which plays a huge part in defining their tone and audience appeal.

Prose fiction

Prose has the wonderful ability to tell us, the reader, what is inside a character's mind or have the character herself tell us, without us ever hearing the actual voice of a character. The *voice* or style of the author is not dependent on the actual voice or dialogue of the characters. Instead, dialogue in prose, not unlike in film and TV, becomes a literary device, a technique among many that enhances the story through tone, revealing character, which can help to advance the plot. Therefore, in fiction prose, it is through written, and subsequently read, language that all of the sensations – sounds, feelings, emotions, visuals, and thoughts – are conveyed.

In television and film scripts, dialogue is the most prominent feature on the page. Certainly, there are the screen directions as well, but when you flip through a script, you mostly see pages filled with dialogue. In prose fiction, it is the opposite, or there might not be any actual dialogue at all. But it is the context of the dialogue within prose that primarily separates it from dramatic writing.

Here's an example of contemporary dialogue from a novel that has the immediacy of a film script, but seems to fit in our inner mind's eye and ear even more as something written and read. It's by Richard Price from his novel *The Whites* (2015, Henry Holt and Company):

> There was no message, only an attached JPEG, Billy opening it to see a flash-lit snap of Curtis Taft lying cuffed and gagged on a wooden floor, his red-dot eyes buzzing from above the fat strip of electrical tape that had been slapped across his mouth. The photo had been sent from Taft's own phone, but Billy had to be an idiot not to guess who the shutterbug was. After reversing back into his spot, he threw the car into park and immediately started to dial.
>
> "What did you do."
>
> "Come and see," Pavlicek said.

"Is he dead?" "Come and see."

"Where are you."

"Fifteen twenty-two Vyse." In the heart of their old precinct, in a building Pavlicek owned.

"Fuck you. Don't move."

"I wouldn't dream of it."

Price, who is also a prominent screen and television writer, is among the best dialogue writers working in prose. You can see that his language has the bite and energy of authenticity, but in this scene, as it's on the phone, it would lose its seamlessness if it were on the screen cutting between two characters, or us seeing one person and overhearing the other through the phone.

Although Price's gritty dialogue itself can be transported to film, the details and information that he contextualizes them around are far less filmic. For example, the prose description, "the photo had been sent from Taft's own phone, but Billy had to be an idiot not to guess who the shutterbug was," is meant to be understood by the reader and couldn't be as precisely conveyed visually or informationally, even by a great actor's performance.

Dialogue in prose fiction can also lean toward more purely literary realms that would be difficult to translate into commercial film or television. An example of this can be read throughout James Joyce's novel *Ulysses* (1922):

—How do you do? the editor said, holding out a hand. Come in. Your governor is just gone.

Lenehan said to all:

—Silence! What opera resembles a railwayline? Reflect, ponder, excogitate, reply.
Stephen handed over the typed sheets, pointing to the title and signature.
—Who? the editor asked.
Bit torn off.
—Mr Garrett Deasy, Stephen said.
—That old pelters, the editor said. Who tore it? Was he short taken?
  On swift sail flaming From storm and south He comes, pale vampire, Mouth to my mouth.
—Good day, Stephen, the professor said, coming to peer over their shoulders. Foot and mouth? Are you turned...?
Bullockbefriending bard.

For less commercial film experiences, dialogue that resembles Joyce's might serve as an inspiration to screenwriters who want to convey a unique, arthouse type of language.

Film dialogue vs. TV dialogue

There is no specific or absolute difference in the actual words used in writing dialogue for film or television. To be clear, when I speak of television, I'm referring primarily to narratives made for viewing on screens other than in a movie theater. This includes narratives from established networks, cable, and prime and pay television, along with digital streaming platforms with content intended to be viewed on computer and mobile device screens in addition to television screens. This being said, even though commercial-free programing and movie-length stand-alone narratives are a part of the new non-movie theater landscape, we mostly associate television-oriented scripted shows with series (limited or ongoing) that are half-hour or one-hour in length and are designed for addictive viewing.

There are, however, some format and structural differences that can, and often do, inform different approaches to dialogue writing for film and TV. The basic formatting of screenplays and television writing have traditionally been slightly different. Television, especially half-hour sitcoms, typically have dialogue written with double spaces between each line, whereas one-hour dramas are written more like film scripts, with single-space dialogue. And in both half-hour and one-hour television, act breaks are denoted. Additionally, in TV scripts, wherever the act ends, the rest of that page remains empty in order to start the new act at the top of the next page. Currently, there tends to be a more homogenized approach with television scripts looking more like film scripts. It seems to depend on the whims of a particular TV showrunner or the standards of a particular production company or network. Though most one-hour and many half-hour scripted TV shows still adhere to "teasers," or "cold opens," and often continue to denote act breaks, there's a greater emphasis for this on shows that will be broken up by commercials.

Since a film's length is fairly finite and typically between 90 and 120 minutes, there is literally less time for character-building exposition, as there is on a television series. In *film*, the dialogue has to be more consciously specific and able to push both the story and the character forward more economically and quickly than a TV series might demand.

Another difference is the half-hour sitcom format in which the rapid-fire style of dialogue specifically trades on non-stop laughs. The dialogue style of continuous verbal set-up-and-joke would be exhausting to sit through for a feature film length of time. But for half-hour sitcoms, it is great.

One of the biggest differences between film and TV is how commercials inform, if not dictate, dramatic content. The need for creating cliffhangers as "outs" before every commercial doesn't affect the actual language used, but it does require inventive and suspenseful content that often requires dialogue explanations or posed questions. This kind of heightened dramatic effect is still needed and prevalent in films, but just not as restricted by the clockwork-like timing that writing around commercials necessitate. It may or may not affect the actual words of dialogue as much as the content of the situations.

This demand for creating periodic heightened plotting has more or less become true for TV writing even in shows without commercials. And of course, we're talking about most premium television and digital platform shows. The need to compel audiences to stay tuned to each moment-to-moment remains the task at hand. And inventive writers use whatever devices that they can to achieve this. Dialogue, then, is an essential tool to this end. Whether it is through employing dialogue with clever histrionics or a unique idiosyncratic voice, the ever-increasing need to attract viewership demands a very high standard of writing.

Historically, film has tended to emphasize a more visual approach toward storytelling with a greater ability to create and convey spectacle on the big screen. Consequently, film, and more clearly, visually oriented films, tend to rely less on dialogue as the primary method for conveying story information. But this is not a singular truism, and the differences, if any between television and film, tend to be informed by content, style, visual enhancements (3D, etc.), and viewing methods (IMAX, etc.). Viewing a film on a movie-theater-sized screen lends itself to displaying nuanced, as well as spectacular, visuals. Enormous screens are more suited for displaying large and visually stunning situations than, say, watching people talking.

But traditional ideas about the differences between TV and film are in flux and always being blurred. Big screen, visually oriented film directors, such as David Fincher and Danny Boyle, have embraced the smaller screen. Look at Fincher's *House of Cards* (2013) or *Mindhunter* (2017), which are dialogue heavy. TV traditionally tends to be "talkier" than films and less visually oriented. But this is not always the case. *Game of Thrones* (2011) anyone? Things are changing.

PART TWO
Tool kits for improving your dialogue

The various approaches, observations, tendencies, and details that are covered in Part Two should be considered as *tools of the trade* for dialogue writing. Tools help us complete tasks and improve the way that we work. Sometimes they are essential, like a wrench for a plumber. But just as it's important to have good tools, it's equally essential that they be used in the right way. A professional brings his tool kit to work, and it's filled with all sorts of devices and appliances for the various tasks at hand. As screen and television writers, there is a huge body of information and tools that professional writers bring to their craft, which goes beyond their honed and earned instincts. The specifics of writing dialogue are often related to tenants of screenwriting as a whole, but this specialty also has additional tools of its own. Some of them are obvious, some of them are practical, and some of them are custom-made. However you view them, consider the contents of a writer's tool kit as something that is always being expanded, changed, and improved.

6

TOOL KIT – WRITING DIALOGUE

Introduction: Tool kit – Writing dialogue

When we talk about the specifics in this chapter and in the rest of Part Two, we need to keep in mind that dialogue is not math. Here, two plus two is not always four. However, when it is not four, we should still be able to *feel* the logic, no matter how oblique, of whatever it is. Keeping this in mind, consider the contents of Part Two "Tool Kits for Improving Your Dialogue," as helpful tendencies, observable traits, and areas of details regarding dialogue that are worth understanding and remembering in film and TV content that you encounter. If applied, it can help raise the quality and timbre of your scripted conversations.

But also remember that just as one can lead the proverbial horse to water, but can't make him drink, we as instructors, coaches, editors, and consultants can only lead a writer toward the specifics of where the work must be done. Coming up with the magic and the ineffable ... cannot be taught. It can be observed and noted, and most important, one can learn where and when it might be needed. There's no repeatable formula or even methodology, per se, for conjuring sparkling dialogue. But with practice, especially practicing what to look and listen for, one can be much more predisposed, and subsequently much more able to catch a "firefly" of talking inspiration, which can illuminate a moment. It just takes a few moments.

The good news is that most working dialogue doesn't rely upon brilliant word usage or quirky, original turns of phrases every time characters open their mouths. There are plenty of professional scripts that have become successful films without any expressly memorable dialogue at all. When you think of most films that you've seen, does the dialogue from them leap forward in your memory? Clearly, for some films and TV shows, the dialogue is very memorable. But the bar is high, and getting higher, for what even constitutes working, or workman-like, dialogue. And being attentive to what follows in this chapter can give you a leg up toward making your dialogue at least appropriate to your narrative. Sometimes we need to create dialogue that simply does not get in the way of what is going on.

Starting – What do you do?

At some point, you just have to jump into the double Dutch jump rope. So this is the moment. You are about to write dialogue. You are about to write words that your characters will speak. Where do you start? What? How? Why? Okay, relax, you've already done this your entire life; you've spoken many times! When you wanted something or needed to tell someone something; when the thoughts in your head somehow became words in your mouth; when, because you felt something – pain, joy, or a myriad of sensations – words erupted without you even thinking about it. The mystery of how thoughts become spoken words might remain a mystery to neurologists but not to us, because we do it all the time!

Dialogue is not written in a vacuum. For most screenwriters, it is among the last parts of the screenwriting process, after the vast majority of the story is suffered over, endlessly considered, and carefully plotted out. And after a trillion decisions have been decided, at least in your mind if not on paper, including locations, names, ages, physical attributes, and specific events. This is also often after a complete outline of the entire narrative has been written out, replete with ample information about every scene and about every important character and where each character is on their transformative arc; and after each scene has been meticulously organized in a way that leads an audience on a complete journey with a satisfying resolution. At least hopefully.

Typically, only then does the actual *writing* commence: the slug lines, the description, and then, as needed, the dialogue. *At least in the beginning, if you can't hear the particular voice of your characters, write dialogue the way that you'd say it in your normal speaking voice.* As you rewrite and revise, you'll be able to punch up your dialogue more consciously using many of the techniques included in this book. Also, as you become more aware of where your dialogue can be enhanced, sharpened, and made more dynamic, that awareness alone can lead you to find better words, language, or sonic alternatives. But by this point, you often already will know, at least in general terms, not only the beginning, middle, and end of your entire story (or episode), and the basic character arcs you're aspiring to create, but also what you need each scene to convey informationally. That is, the basic bottom-line information that is required for another person to comprehend the logic of the story. And, like a puppeteer, you begin to manipulate the actions and dialogue of your characters and make them say words that you feel they would say to convey information or *sentiments* that you sense are required.

To illustrate this, imagine writing a script in which you want to introduce the audience to a family, but you don't exactly know what they'll say. You know it's not an important scene beyond establishing this family; it's not hugely dramatic or heavy, and you want it to be simple and fairly realistic in order to set the tone. Of course, you'd love it to be entertaining, hopefully to push the story and character development forward, but you still can't quite *hear* what the family should talk about. One useful way to solve this problem is to look at the overall story, what it's about, and then come up with a way to speak about it through a story or metaphoric situation. Here's a great example from the acclaimed film *The Farewell* (2019), written and directed by Lulu Wang. It's the story of a family that goes on a trip to say goodbye to their beloved grandmother, who is the only person that doesn't know that she only has a few weeks to live. In the following scene, we meet the family for the first time, sans the grandmother, and the father tells a joke that essentially is the entire plot of the rest of the film we're about to see.

```
                 HAIYAN (O.S.) (prelap)
     ... and one day the wife goes out of town.
     When she returns, her husband greets her
     right away, and he says, 'honey your cat
     is dead.'

INT. WANG FAMILY HOME, DINING ROOM (QUEENS, NYC) -
NIGHT

HAIYAN WANG (late 50's), also known as DAD, smiles
with self assurance as family and friends anticipate
the rest of his joke. Billi watches her father
adoringly, sipping brandy around the remains of their
dinner.

                 HAIYAN
     The wife gets very upset, you know? She
     says to her husband, how can you be so
     insensitive? You just tell me so abruptly
     like this?

Despite his slight Chinese accent, Haiyan's a natural
storyteller.
```

                          HAIYAN (CONT'D).
              Her husband is you know, confused! He says
              to his wife... OK, how do you want me to
              tell you in the future? She says, "You have
              to not be so direct. It's too sudden. You
              have to, you know, be more gentle in
              delivering the news. For example, ease me
              in with something like 'Listen, honey...
              your cat... it got on the roof...'"

A few scattered chuckles from the table. JIAN LU, also
known as MOM (late 50's), enters with plates of cake.

                          KATHY
              Oh my gosh, I'm stuffed. I don't know if
              I have room for dessert.

Haiyan is slightly irritated by the interruption.

                          HAIYAN
              Come, sit down...

                          BILLI
              Come, Mom.

                          HAIYAN
              Where was I? Oh right... A few months go
              by. The wife goes out of town again. When
              she returns home, her husband's there to
              greet her again. This time, he learned his
              lesson. When his wife comes through the
              door, he says, "Listen, honey, you know,
              your Mom... she got on the roof..."

The table bursts into laughter. Even Billi and Jian
chuckle, despite having heard the joke a million
times.

Working it all out before you start writing might be the most common way screen
and TV writers work, but there is no ironclad rule. There are some screenwriters who discover many of the aspects discussed earlier during the actual process
of writing, including dialogue. And even with meticulous planning, sometimes,
while writing dialogue, characters increasingly reveal themselves. Words, sentences, and ideas literally appear that you didn't plan or expect to write; that
you didn't anticipate that your characters would even say. Some might call it
"channeling" your character, and if it works for you, surprises you in a good way,

and even leads your story in new directions, it can be a fantastic, unexpected gift. However, if in the cold light of revisions you realize that what you wrote doesn't work for your story or fit your character you can always nix it. This kind of surprise channeling doesn't always work this way every time you're writing dialogue, and not for every character or for every writer. But somehow, through the mysterious process of putting words in characters' mouths, there is a great propensity for characters to say things that are surprising even to the writer. Be open to it. Go with it. You can always delete it.

Intention – What do you want?

This should be the first thing that you think about as you approach writing any dialogue for any character: what do you want? And I'm referring to the two yous: you the writer and you the character. Not only does the dialogue sound listless and without energy when the *wants* are not clear, it is also torturous to write. We've spoken about *wants* before, especially in relation to *needs*. We've looked at their similarity to *goals* and *inner goals* of a character, both immediately and throughout the length of the entire story. Each of these concepts is hugely important for you to know either before you begin writing or while you're in the process of writing. Because, as stated, sometimes, as you are literally in the act of writing dialogue, you find yourself writing words that you didn't even expect. If this occurs in service of your characters intended goals, wants, and needs, then that is where the surprises are likely to occur. Neurologically, the mind works that way; we never actually know precisely what our next thought will be. Our minds perpetually generate thoughts, so be open to what you find and think while you're writing. Once you begin to inhabit a character, in some strange way, you might be able to channel her or his actual thoughts.

We, and our characters, don't always say what we want directly. Sometimes, we say it obliquely, or even say the opposite.

There are many ways, for example, to say "I love you," and many of them don't include the word "love" or even its literal sentiment. A person, frustrated by their lover and their inability to express their amorous feelings might say "you really drive me crazy" or even "I hate you!" But if they smile while they say it, or whisper it while they're embracing, even pejorative words can take on their opposite meaning. "Yes" doesn't always mean yes either.

Structure, shape, and pace

Just as there is a discernible structure and shape to scenes and the entire narrative, there is also a similarly discernable structure and shape to dialogue. However, dialogue is considerably more flexible and axiomatic. The greatest similarity between the two is that they both begin and end with something occurring in between. Of course, this wouldn't exactly hold for near-monosyllabic replies like "uh huh," "OK," "nope," and "why not?" to name but a few. But just as in scene writing in which you wouldn't want to climax the scene in the beginning, you should also withhold the most pertinent or most dynamic information within the dialogue banter itself. Pace the most charged information so that it is baked into a reply or speech that compels us and the other characters to listen.

So for example, if one character asks another, "Did you sleep with my wife?" then, in answering this charged question, you, the writer, are suddenly in complete control of everyone's rapt attention, everyone being the character who asked the question and the audience who also wants to know the answer. Realize that a part of dialogue writing is pacing information. If, after being asked that question, the character lapses into a parable, an anecdotal story, or answers mysteriously, we will hang on to every word. But pacing also means knowing when to answer the question.

The do's, don'ts, and exceptions

Despite various adamant opinions, very few rules about writing are absolutely ironclad and binary enough to divide into definitive do's and don'ts. Elmore Leonard touts that when writing prose, one should *never* use a verb other than "said" to carry dialogue ("Watch out!" he said). And if you read his work, you'll see that he never breaks this rule. But others, including other incredibly good and famous writers, do break it all the time. It's not that rules are made to be broken, but where art is concerned, rules are most beneficial if they are understood as wise observations that help codify the most efficient paths toward positive results. With that in mind, consider the following observations.

Always keep in mind

These are among the bedrock, foundational aspects, if not tenants, of writing dialogue that it would be a good idea to integrate into your automatic thinking whenever you're working on dialogue. The goal is for these notions to become an integral part of your writing intuition, and through repeated study, observation of them in action, application, and experimentation, they will raise your dialogue-writing instinct. *Note*: Many of the same aspects for writing strong dialogue pertain equally, and often similarly, toward creating a strong structure and plot of your entire story.

- *Is your dialogue moving the story forward, illuminating character and/or entertaining?* If not, why is it there?
- *What are the wants, needs, goals, and inner goals of your character?* Consider this before writing each scene, and especially before writing the dialogue of each character, because humans answer these questions in the darndest ways. Unconscious or suppressed urges continue to leak out of people's minds and color their everyday communication. This is where your creativity as a writer can be unleashed and you can find unique and even odd traits or bits of information that betray a character's otherwise more secretive,

unexamined self. And although you want to ask these questions regarding the immediate scene at hand, it'll be of great value if you also know the answers for each character regarding their place in the story as a whole. *Wants* and *needs* often pertain to the immediate situation regarding the present scene and what's happening at that moment. But this is not always the case. For example, right now, a character might *want* ice cream, but *needs* some nourishing food. Beyond the present, she *wants* a Ferrari, but she *needs* a car. Goals are considered what the main character aspires to achieve by the end of the story. *Inner goals* are those unconscious or less conscious motivations for achieving the goal. Let's say a character's goal is to win the spelling bee, but her unconscious or less conscious inner goal is to please her dad. Although this was discussed in previous chapters, it's of paramount importance that you understand how these impulses (wants, needs, goals, inner goals) directly affect strong dialogue. Remember, what comes out of our mouths are manifestations of our insides.

Here's a good example of all sorts of inner, even surprising and otherwise undisclosed aspects of character bleeding into what could have been a straightforward conversation. In this case, in two snippets of a scene from the Academy Award–winning script *Good Will Hunting* (1997), intellectually gifted Will *wants* to disparage the psychologist, Sean, into declining to take him on as a patient. Will sincerely *needs* psychological help. And Sean *wants* to help Will, but Sean also *needs* to be challenged to change aspects of himself. Here, Will is looking at the books on shelf:

```
INT. SEAN'S OFFICE - DAY

Sean's office is comfortable. Books are stacked against
the wall. There is a PAINTING on the wall behind Sean.
Sean is seated behind a desk.

                    SEAN
          Hello, Will. I'm Sean Maguire.

A smile crosses Will's face as he walks to his chair
and sits. He lights a cigarette. Sean continues to
watch him. Finally-


                    SEAN
          Where are you from in Southie?

                    WILL
          Did you buy all these books retail, or do
          you send away for like a "shrink kit" that
          comes with all these volumes included?
```

                    SEAN
        Have you read all these books, Will?

                    WILL
        Probably not.

                    SEAN
                (indicating a shelf)
        How about the ones on that shelf?

Will's eyes flicker up to the shelf for an instant.

                    WILL
        Yeah, I read those.

                    SEAN
        What did you think?

                    WILL
        I'm not here for a fuckin' book report.
        They're your books, why don't you read 'em?

                    SEAN
        I did.

                    WILL
        That must have taken you a long time.

                    SEAN
        Yeah, it did take me a long time.

Later in the scene, Will analyzes the painting on the
wall.

                    WILL
        Maybe you were in the middle of a storm, a
        big fuckin' storm -- the waves were crashing
        over the bow, the Goddamned mast was
        about to snap, and you were crying for the
        harbor. So you did what you had to do, to
        get out. Maybe you became a psychologist.

                    SEAN
        Maybe you should be a patient and sit down.

                    WILL
        Maybe you married the wrong woman.

                    SEAN
        Watch your mouth.

                    WILL
     That's it isn't it? You married the wrong woman.
     She leave you? Was she bangin' someone else?

Sean is walking slowly towards Will.

                    WILL
     How are the seas now, D--

In a flash, Sean has Will by the throat. Will is
helpless.

                    SEAN
     If you ever disrespect my wife
     again ... I will end you.

                    WILL
     Time's up.

The wants and needs of this scene ooze out of the dialogue just as the greater *goals* and *inner goals* of both characters also bleed into what they say. In this case, although Will's overall *goal* was to get through court-appointed therapy to avoid jail, his *inner goal* was to free himself from his troubled past, which, by the film's conclusion he begins to do. And Sean's goal is to help Will, but his inner goal is to move beyond mourning his deceased wife. You can see how similar the goals and inner goals are to wants and needs. But, it is the wants and needs that more immediately inform the scene.

- *Conflicts and tension are more dynamic than static conversation.* Strive to find or create tension within the dialogue. Aside from actual arguments, or being in the presence of potential violence, characters can toss up all sorts of obstacles in a conversation that causes tension, which are more fun and compelling to listen to. For example, if you ask your friend to hand you a glass of water and she says "no," the process of finding out why can open up all sorts of revealing possibilities. It can be as simple and benign as "because the last time I gave you a glass of water, you didn't drink it," or more seriously, "because I first need to get something off my chest." And this type of "tension-creating" interplay can transpire within your scene, even when it's about something else entirely.
- *As real or authentic as your dialogue may or may not be, it's all performative.* Don't forget to hear it from the audience's point of view and entertain us. Do you remember the dialogue from *Moonstruck* (1987)? It was purposely operatic.
- *If it can be communicated visually, including via a character's expression, it might be best unsaid.* This is especially true if the character is not an overly talkative type of person. And the opposite is also true: when a talkative person is suddenly quiet or unresponsive, it can be very effective. Sometimes scenes can be more powerful and emotional with fewer words spoken.

- *Specificity rules. Genericism lies flat.* This is true not just for adjectives and adverbs, but also for nouns and any word that can be stated more uniquely. "I saw a green car and I felt bad" is quite generic. "I saw a hopped-up 1970 Pontiac GTO convertible and it made me wanna puke" is better. It has more energy, gives more to visualize, and reveals more about the character speaking. *Note*: Like adding spices while cooking, a little goes a long way. Every single line of your script does not need to be earth-shatteringly unique in order for your script to zing. Here's one of many terrific examples of great language in the wonderfully written *Booksmart* (2019):

> MOLLY
> Oh my God. Your crush on him
> perplexes me.
>   AMY
> I can't help it. I'm drawn to him.
> It's like a - a uterine pull. I have
> no control over it. Also he was also
> nice to me one day.

Uterine pull? Perfect.

And here, again from *Juno* (2007), is among the great specificities of screenwriting, something that Bleeker says to Juno:

> BLEEKER
> Like I'd marry you! You would be the
> meanest wife of all time. And anyway,
> I know you weren't bored that day
> because there was a lot of stuff on
> TV. The Blair Witch Project was on
> Starz, and you were like, "Oh, I
> want to watch this, but we should make
> out instead. La la la."

He could've just left it after "there was a lot of stuff on TV." But to go on and be so achingly specific saying, "The Blair Witch Project was on Starz" is what lifts this moment to another level entirely. Yes, many viewers might miss the reference, but it doesn't matter, since you can feel the intensity of his brain working. And for the core audience of *Juno*, it's a pure delight.

And then …

These are trusted observations that you'd also be wise to include in your knowledge base of writing dialogue. They might not initially be among your greatest concerns, *but especially as you revise your work*, these should be kept in constant consideration:

- *Avoid expository dialogue.* Make sure that characters tell each other information that is logically appropriate and new for them to learn. *Not* simply information that the writer wants to convey to the audience. When dialogue starts feeling awkward, burdened, and even slightly unnatural, check to see that it is not overly expository.
- *Strive for authentic language.* This includes word choices and sentence structure. People don't always speak in complete sentences. Sometimes, they stop midway through a line. They pause. They make mistakes. Use words, terms, and argot that fit the characters' world.
- *Start as late in the conversation as you can and get out as early as possible.* Not that this is always possible, but consider where you enter a conversation as a decision that can inform both the energy of the dialogue and its authenticity. When you consider overheard conversations, it is often amazing how little you have to hear to get a sense of what is being spoken about. Entering later can help to rid sentences that are dull, lead-ups, and expository. Of course, as said previously, this isn't always possible; we might have to watch two people meeting before we see them speak. In this case, it would be impossible to start their conversation any later. But you can end their conversation before they finish talking. You can leave the scene even though it's implied that the characters will still be continuing to be with each other. *Note*: If you end dialogue before conversations are fully resolved, it tends to push the audience's attention toward the future or fill them with anticipation regarding the less-resolved outcome of where that conversation will lead. Even on a simple level, if characters are speaking and trying to decide where they should go after work, rather than end the scene after they've argued and identified the specific restaurant, it's stronger if we cut out of the scene with them questioning where they should go. This way, we too want to know the answer and will be surprised when it's revealed in the next or future scene. Leaving the audience unresolved helps to compel the narrative forward.
- *Subtext often works better than text.* Be careful not to write too literally, directly, or "on the nose" too often. Though sometimes a rose is a rose, when people express themselves, they are so often unaware of how many emotions and judgments they are hiding, suppressing, or avoiding. And they speak in subtext, indirectly talking about things that they can't, are unwilling, or are afraid to confront. For example, if someone is angry with another person, it is rarely expressed directly. Maybe it's said through subtextually replying to that person in an uncharacteristically negative or sullen way. Maybe it's through refusing the person something that ordinately wouldn't be refused. Maybe it's by inserting insults and put-downs into the conversation, subtly or not so subtly degrading the person, or something that the person likes. There are a million subtextual ways that people express their unhappiness or anger without ever

saying "I'm pissed at you!" And by finding those ways, you are making your characters' dialogue more real, compelling, and relatable. Be smart about how characters express or avoid their feelings, wants, and needs. Even if they are therapied-out and speak in ultra-self-conscious declarations, they still might be either missing the truth or deluding themselves.

- *But there is a time for direct, honest, sincere textual communication.* Avoid squandering sincere, non-ironic communication. When it arrives at the right time, it has great power.
- *Beware of repeating information unless that's an essential trait of the character.* Scripted dialogue is relentless in its economy. If information or even words are repeated within a character's speech, or even within the conversation, the audience, or the reader of the script, keenly picks up on it. It can feel ponderous and unprofessional. Aside from learning to trust your audience, there are other ways to signpost things that you feel are important and don't want the audience to miss. Among these are the use of underlining, capitalizing, and italicizing of words or whole sentences that you want to emphasize in the dialogue or scene descriptions.
- *Trust your audience, the way that you'd trust a ten-year-old.* Kids today are smart and sophisticated. But they're still kids – restless, forgetful, and inattentive. Be patient and explain it to them in simple terms. And do the same for us, the audience, as well. That doesn't mean being patronizing. It means being clear and patient.
- *Use metaphors and story examples.* When characters tell amusing or interesting anecdotes and stories, we listen.
- *Make sure every character doesn't sound the same or speak in the same manner, in terms of length of sentences, word usage, content, mood, and rhythms.* Especially avoid characters speaking back and forth in similarly long blocks of dialogue.
- *Strive for varied and/or syncopated rhythms between characters.*
- *Be aware of where, within the dialogue, each character reveals charged information.* Learn to pace charged or surprising information in order to control tension. You don't want to give away the most charged, surprising, or important information too early on in a conversation, unless you have equally or even more important information still to come.
- *Avoid literally spelling out each word phonetically in dialect or patois.* Mark Twain did, screenwriter's don't. Spell out the literal sound of a few choice words when your character speaks in order to give the feeling of the language, accent, or style that your character expresses. But this isn't necessary for every word that they speak. Let the actor fill it in throughout. (See the section "Colloquial Language and Vernacular" in Chapter Seven.)
- *Remove words to make your dialogue more distinctive.* A quick method to make dialogue pop and distinctive is by subtracting words. This can immediately help dialogue feel less mannered. Many lines of dialogue can use being pruned by at least the first word or two. Similarly, the last sentence, words, or exchange often is better left unsaid or hanging.

Obvious, but you can't hear it enough

Like when learning anything new, repetition is essential. Along those lines, the following might be obvious, but like so many obvious aspects of life, we tend to take them for granted. Don't. Review these like repeating a mantra:

- *Dialogue should be purposeful and there for a reason.* It should advance the story forward with information and/or reveal in greater depth something about a character. Not only is it forwarding and facilitating the story, but ideally it should inform the character's conscious or unconscious personal agendas and intentions.
- *It's not always about "realistic" dialogue. It's about appropriate, authentic, and entertaining dialogue.* Just because you actually heard something spoken a certain way, doesn't make it necessarily suitable or authentic to the moment.
- *Real conversation has mindless non sequiturs, but if it is scripted it must be purposeful.* Often during conversation, when either a speaker or the one they're conversing with suddenly changes subject without warning, it's mindless, innocent, and often the result of overenthusiasm or limited attention. In scripted dialogue, it's either a character trait or, more tellingly, an indication of avoidance.
- *Be careful not to overuse character names in your dialogue.* When we speak to each other, we mostly don't say the other person's name. We do sometimes, as in "So, whataya think, John?" We might on occasion mention their name, but in scripted dialogue, more than once in a conversation sounds stilted and artificial. Unless that's the point of conveying a certain kind of awkward character.
- *The way a character talks is the way that her mind works.* Clearly? Logically? Scattered? Nonlinear?
- *Be sensitive to stereotypical language, especially gender and racial tropes.*
- *Avoid overwriting speeches and rambling conversations.*
- *Avoid generic words and terms.*
- *Avoid the mundane* unless *it's funny, quirky, or revealingly mundane.*
- *Don't forget to contextualize dialogue with narrative descriptions.*
- *Through dialogue, express characters' moods and desires beyond the informational goals of the scene.*
- *Dialogue-wise: Less is often more.* Though this is a general rule, be careful not to overload dialogue with too much information or data.
- *Strive to create surprise.* Be it in a surprising word, turn of phrase, or tidbit of information.
- *Be aware of the power dynamics between characters as they converse.*
- ***There are no rules if it sounds right.***

7

TOOL KIT – SPECIFICITY

- Introduction: Tool kit – Specificity
- Nouns
- Modifiers
- Unique words
- Authentic and technical words
- Colorful words
- Colloquial language and vernacular

Introduction: Tool kit – Specificity

A whole chapter devoted to the subject of specificity in dialogue should suggest to you the importance of this concept. But what are we talking about – being specific? Isn't that obvious? Yes, it is obvious and it is still too often overlooked, neglected, and forgotten. There are a trillion examples all around us, but really honing in on specifics cannot only make all the difference in great dialogue, but also reveal aspects of your characters that you were not even aware you didn't know. Can you imagine this line from the Beatles song *A Day in the Life*, "Now they know how many holes it takes to fill the Albert Hall," if they had said "Now they know how many holes it takes to fill the concert hall"? It's minor, yes, and possible, sure, but not as good, strong, or perfectly specific. It also wouldn't be as personal, meaningful, and colorful. The value of specificity cannot be understated.

When you begin to recognize specificity in dialogue and observe how it makes you feel, you'll begin to understand its value. It connects us to the character speaking in a unique way; it tantalizes our brain and draws us into listening more closely. But since the notion of parsing every specific word usage can be overwhelming, the following pages will focus on nouns, adjectives, and adverbs as they are commonly used in dialogue. *The idea is to first become aware of these kinds of words and their power to enhance dialogue. And then, consider your ability to find even stronger word choices as a powerful tool in your tool kit for raising the general caliber of your dialogue writing.*

Nouns

The common definition for a noun is a word that functions as a name for a person, place, or thing. And although there are more complex subcategories, including proper nouns, concrete nouns, and abstract nouns, for our purposes in writing dialogue, let's just consider the common definition. And as simple as this may sound, in our normal talking, we often don't have the specific names of things. Instead, we use generic names. We might say "the car" as opposed to "the 1974 Jaguar XKE." But in conversation, when someone does use a specific term or word, it rarely fails to impress us. Though sometimes it might evoke the opposite response, calling attention to an obnoxious know-it-all, either way, it is noticeable, even if just felt. And since scripted dialogue is not about realism as much as it is about our aspirations of realism, when characters pull specific names of otherwise generic things seemingly out of the air, we love it. And this cuts across all aspects of character types and intelligence.

Whether it's a marginal hitman in *Pulp Fiction* (1994) talking about the very specific "Royale with Cheese" or a working-class heroin addict in *Trainspotting* (1996) describing fantastical "brilliant gold taps, virginal white marble, a seat carved from ebony, a cistern full of Chanel No. 5, and a flunky handing me pieces of raw silk toilet roll," or a genius young Ivy Leaguer in *The Social Network* (2010) expressing his desire to join "the Porcellian Club," the specificities these characters espouse are what helps to elevate their dialogue, uniqueness, and memorability. And it doesn't matter whether everyone in the audience knows what a "Royale with Cheese" is, what "Chanel No. 5" smells like, or what on earth the "the Porcellian Club" is. We intuitively understand that the characters know what they are talking about and this fact alone makes their dialogue all the more compelling for us to listen to.

Modifiers

Some literary writers and teachers are bullish about being especially sparing in one's use of modifiers. Stephen King famously wrote in his memoir, *On Writing: A Memoir of the Craft*, that "the road to hell is paved with adverbs." He is not alone. And for prose, it's a caution worth noting. Typically, modifiers are those words that modify, clarify, and enhance our nouns and verbs. The conventional wisdom is that writers who rely on modifiers are too lazy to find more precise words that don't require additional description. But in dialogue, just as in our daily conversations, we use modifiers all the time, even if they are often quite mundane. "Look at that big house." The adjective "big" is the modifier in this sentence that helps describe the house. True, you might say "look at that mansion," and then you might not need to further describe its size. But in normal conversation, we are rarely so precise. And even though throughout this chapter we will be stressing the importance of being precise and specific with your word usage, we are equally stressing that they must also sound appropriately authentic to the characters and the world that they inhabit.

Without being either too pedantic or inauthentically precise, through the creative use of modifiers, we can turn everyday language into punchier, more memorable dialogue. "Look at that humongous house!" already sounds punchier. We also often use lazy adverbs to further modify adjectives or verbs: In the statement "look at the very big house," "very" is the adverb modifier of "big." How big? Very. And again, this is often how we actually speak. But if we consider a more unique modifier, it quickly lifts the line to "look at that crazy-big pad" or "check out that crazy-big jimongous house!" Feel free to invent words if they convey your meaning, and if they fit your character. Not every character would say "check out that crazy-big jimongous house!"

The point of being creative in your use of modifiers is not only to make your dialogue more vibrant, but also to help inform the characters who speak them. Here are some wonderful, inspirational examples of modifiers . First, from *Fleabag* (2016):

> FLEABAG (to camera)
> The only thing harder than telling your
> super-high-powered-richanorexic-super-
> sister you have run out of money is
> having to ask her to bail you out.

Wow. The character Fleabag is certainly not holding back on her feelings about her sister. And aside from this passage being delightfully cutting, it also both describes Fleabag's true feelings and lets us know the magnitude of her inner rage.

In *Booksmart* (2019), a single, self-consciously placed modifier tells us reams of information about how clueless our two lead high school seniors, Molly and Amy, are:

> AMY
> C'mon, we've done everything you told
> us to. We got new looks, we've been
> going out.
>
> MOLLY
> We've made a laudable effort.

```
                JULIE
Stop using words like that, for Christ's
sake. You think a boy's going to date
someone who made a laudable effort?
```

How many high school seniors would say "laudable effort"? Molly could have just said "we've made an effort" or even "we've worked really hard," but the word "laudable" so perfectly tells us about Molly and Amy, how they're crazy overachievers, while slightly tingling our ears. It's at the same time out of place, brilliantly pretentious, and altogether wonderful – exactly like Molly and Amy.

Single words can elevate passages of dialogue. Here's a quirky receptionist at a women's clinic in *Juno* (2007):

```
             PUNK RECEPTIONIST
I need you to fill these out, both
sides. And don't skip the hairy
details. We need to know about every
score and every sore.
```

"Hairy details" is funny, gross, and accurately fits the punk receptionist and the birth control clinic's style. And we totally understand the meaning even if "hairy" is not a word typically used in this context, let alone in a medical clinic.

At first, write your dialogue like how you would hear it in your mind. Let it freely flow out of your head and write it conversationally. As you go back and look it over, you'll suddenly see a million opportunities to use or add creative and unique modifiers. Common modifiers are opportunities for better, incisive, and dynamic ones.

Unique words

Of course, anything specific will be, unto itself, *unique*. But I'm trying to draw your attention to what unique means in terms of dialogue, which includes specific word and concept usage that is unique to the character who speaks them. Although in the next chapter we will more specifically address "characters" and how understanding them can help you find their own innate and singular dialogue, for now, let's just look at some examples of nouns and how they are particular to the people who speak them. Inevitably, there will be some overlap between concepts such as *specific/unique* and the other categories that we will be considering that follow this one. As a good place to start, let's look at the vocabulary used by the two lovable and brilliant high school losers from *Booksmart*:

```
              AMY
No, of course not. I'm just considering
the ethical implications of driving to
school when there's an oil crisis.
```

> MOLLY
> All the seniors drive to school.
>
> AMY
> Which is precisely the problem! It's
> groupthink. We're at the brink of an
> environmental holocaust, and we -

Although technically some of the terms addressed earlier consist of both nouns and adjectives modifying them, these terms speak to both their unique nature and how seamlessly they flow from equally unique characters. Who speaks about "ethical implications," "groupthink," or "environmental holocaust," let alone high schoolers in a comedy? The answer is wonderful characters created by writers who are clearly desiring for us, the audience, to *get* who these girls are. Without a doubt, there are certainly teenagers who speak this way and are concerned about these issues. And most likely, they are sincere about their concerns, just as we have no doubt that Molly and Amy are serious about these issues too. But being that this is a comedy, we also intuit that their mature "concerns" have somewhat obfuscated their basic awareness about nearly all things *teenager-related*. Maybe it even thwarted their awareness by relying on these worldly concerns as a defense against dealing with the normal vicissitudes of teenage life. Molly and Amy can't help but to use this kind of language in their everyday conversation; it oozes out of them. In many respects, that is what the whole film is about: ultrabright, worldly concerned young women who are attempting to make up for everything they've missed in their high school experience in one big night. At least in this example, the words chosen are not earth-shatteringly unique, per se, but they are voiced by unique teenagers. Surprising context then, as well as word usage itself, goes a long way toward creating uniqueness.

Authentic and technical words

It seems obvious that in narratives that specifically deal with STEM-related or adjacent stories, one would want to use the actual technical words that are common to that world. Here's Richard, a software designer, from *Silicon Valley* (2014):

> RICHARD
> I wrote almost every line of code in
> Pied Piper. Every function, every class,
> every library.

I haven't heard mundane words such as "function," "class," and "library" used in the context of coding. I haven't been privy to coder shoptalk. Frankly, I don't have a clue what he's talking about, but it doesn't matter. Richard speaks with authority and therefore, I believe him. These are fairly benign terms, but we also love to hear the gobbledygook words and technobabble common to science fiction. From the beloved television series *Star Trek* (1966), we effortlessly accept mumbo-jumbo words and terms as though they were commonplace vocabulary:

>   SCOTTY
> I've got bad news, Captain. The entire
> dilithium crystal converter assembly
> is fused.

Divert auxiliary power to the deflectors! Remove the positronic brain! Beware of the tachyon pulses! All of these wonderfully techno-sounding terms dot the entire landscape of sci-fi and superhero genres. It's interesting to note that some of the words are actual terms, loosely related to scientific concepts but with entirely different meanings. Feel free to make up words if they sound real. That is what screen and TV writers have always done. The point here is that by using actual technological terms or technological-sounding terms, writers foster authenticity within the narrative.

But technological terminology should not only be used in sci-fi or tech-related stories. In every narrative, whenever a specific niche, subgroup, or unique world is evoked, there is an opportunity for specific terminology. Whether it's the technical language used in the NFL (*audibles, scrimmage, capology,* etc.), or the jargon used within the world of construction (*plumb, toggle, mud tape,* etc.), characters who use these words are given immediate authority, which helps us to suspend our disbelief.

Of course in police *procedurals*, we have become accustomed to the hardboiled lingo of the genre, and we miss it if it doesn't wind its way into cop-speak: *perps, code-four, negative, copy that,* etc. But again, any character in any situation who uses technical terms appropriately automatically gains a certain amount of stature in our eyes. When we first meet Doc and Carol as they playfully bicker while involved in shooting practice at the beginning of crime drama *The Getaway* (1994), Carol doesn't simply say "I like that big gun." Instead, she says, "This P.P.K.S. is a sweet little weapon." And we instantly take her seriously. In this world, she's immediately a bona fide player.

Clearly, appropriate use of technical terms can lend credibility and authenticity to any dialogue, just as inappropriate, obvious, or ostentatious misuse/overuse can create the opposite effect.

Colorful words

Listening for, and then being able to access or create colorful words, can also boost otherwise ordinary dialogue. But what are *colorful words*? They're words that pop out of normal conversation, like brightly colored objects that grab our attention within an otherwise fairly neutral visual setting. They are words and terms that enter our ears and tickle our brains. The sounds of words can make them colorful, just as unique context or odd usage can also cause them to stand out. For a good example, look at this single passage from a store clerk in the film *Juno*:

> ROLLO
> This is your third test today, Mama Bear. Your eggo is preggo, no doubt about it!

The words "mama" or "bear," just as the term "Mama Bear" might be slightly colorful as words unto themselves that we use as an affectionate name for a protective mom. But when applied to a diminutive sixteen-year-old girl who we are just learning is pregnant, it skews its normal context and tickles our brains. Less out of context, but equally colorful are the words "eggo" and "preggo." Both words are sonic distortions of real words that are seamlessly recognizable and are colorful for how playful their sounds make otherwise serious words appear light.

Aside from the fun of this dialogue, the humorous oddness of a store clerk actually speaking this way also creates a singular tone. Once we accept that this store clerk is a real person within the world of this film, we allow ourselves to enter a tonality in which quirky things can happen. Indeed, *Juno* is filled with wondrous, whimsical things even as it navigates through a serious story.

Another example is one from the film *Superbad* (2007). Even though this excerpt is filled with expletives spewed from a high school senior's mouth, the words themselves are less unique but colorful nonetheless:

> SETH
> I mean, what are we going to tell the girls? "Sorry, we couldn't do what we promised because we're dickless incompetents!" We'll never get laid because of that little ass-fuck. How did he get into State?! He's got shit for brains! Shit! How else can we get liquor?

Here, the whole passage is shiny and colorful: "Dickless incompetents," "little ass-fuck," "shit for brains!" Yes, expletives tend to be *loud* and colorful words. They are typically spoken with vehemence. But the key is to use them creatively, and when you succeed at that, it can raise the entire amusement of what's being said. Concurrently, it can widen our understanding and increase our empathy with the characters speaking them. Vivid, animated words tickle and amuse us, but in excess, like too much sugar, they can alienate us and leave a less-than-desirable taste in our mouths.

Colloquial language and vernacular

Since film and television shows often depict contemporary society, it's optimal for scripted dialogue to authentically reflect everyday, casual, and informal modes of speaking. It's interesting to note just how fast an audience will detect the falseness of everyday language when used incorrectly. Being tone-deaf to how people really converse can instantly sever our connection to the characters and the entire narrative. Of course, if one's intent is to portray an awkward, out-of-touch character, then it can be effective. *Colloquial language* is considered the linguistic style used for casual communication, idioms of speech as opposed to formal or what's considered "proper" speech. It's how an average family converses while sitting around their dinner table. For example, it's more common and realistic today for one friend to say to another "What's up?" than it is to say "How do you do?" And what's considered casual conversation today will be different than that from the 1950s or any other time. Just as what's considered informal speech will also be different for different cultures and subgroups of society.

Within the scope of colloquial conversation, there might also be specific language, terms, idioms, and words used by specialized groups that we'll call their *vernacular*. The term vernacular describes the particular language unique to a singular group or subgroup of people. We can use the term vernacular to describe the specific language that mathematicians, or any other subset of people who use specific terminologies, might employ in their *working conversations*. But when we speak of a particular vernacular, we are more commonly using it to describe the language and modalities of daily speech within specific groups. As a screenwriter, it's important to get those specifics accurate, at least in spirit. The screenwriter and novelist Richard Price has been known to invent slang that his characters speak. To be clear, vernacular language includes all forms of slang, jargon, patois, and dialects, as well as idioms, expressions, and contractions of words. It's what and *how* characters speak. Do they make contractions out of words that other groups wouldn't? Do they cut off consonants such as say "wah?" instead of "what?"

In novels, it is much more common to spell out the exact phonetic sound of the words that characters speak. Mark Twain and William Faulkner immediately come to mind, and it takes a bona fide effort to hear how each word sounds in your mind and what they are actually saying. Here's an example of Jim's sound of speech from Twain's novel *The Adventures of Huckleberry Finn* (1884): "I doan' want to go fool'n 'long er no wrack. We's doin' blame' well, en we better let blame' well alone, as de good book says. Like as not dey's a watchman on dat wrack."

If the preceding passage was in a film or TV script it might look closer to this:

```
                    JIM
      I don't wanna go foolin' 'round on
      that wreck. We're doin' fine without
```

> it, and let's leave well enough alone,
> like the Bible says. Besides, more
> likely than not there's guards
> protecting it.

In TV and film script, we strive for clear, easy to read and understand dialogue. If a character has a lot to say in an extremely stylized or phonetically unique manner, like in the preceding example, it is common to spell out a few key words close to the way that you envision them being spoken. You can assume that the reader, and subsequently the actor, will fill in the same sounds and accents throughout the rest of the passage. Again, there are no absolutes, but especially if you're a new screen or TV writer, you'll want to make the reading process of your script as easy as possible.

Vernacular is not monolithic. Urban American street vernacular, just as Southern Cajun vernacular, can still have infinite nuances, differences, and subtleties within them. Slang and patois vary and mutate with changes in time and location. If one is not confidently familiar with a specific vernacular, the professional script writer does copious research. This often means embedding oneself in a group in order to hear their cadences and specific word choices. If it's from another era or culture, then copious reading of novels from or about that group, culture, or time in history is needed. Especially if you are not an expert in representing a specific vernacular, it's best to err on minimum examples of authenticities and again rely on the reader and actor to fill in the rest. The last thing you want to do is to render characters incompetent or less intelligent, if they are not meant to be, by inauthentic or misrepresentative use of their vernacular.

Here are a few examples of colloquial language used in film. The first is from the film version of the theatrical musical *My Fair Lady* (1964). The entire plot and theme of the movie revolves around an attempt to transform a Cockney working-class girl, Eliza Doolittle, into someone who can pass for a cultured member of high society, starting with "correcting" her speech. It's nearly a primer for looking at how sound-specific dialogue representing a specific group, in this case early twentieth-century working class Cockney, is configured on a page of script:

>   HIGGINS
> Say your vowels.
>
>   ELIZA
> I know me vowels. I knew
> 'em before I come.
>
>   HIGGINS
> If you know them, say them.
>
>   ELIZA
> Ahyee, e, iyee, ow, you.

```
                    HIGGINS
      A,  E,  I,  O,  U.

                    ELIZA
      That's what I said. Ahyee, e,
      iyee, ow, you. That's what I've
      said for three days an' I won't
      no more.
```

Even though many of Eliza's words are phonetically written out, it is still very clear on the page what she is saying and what she means. Clarity is the key.

Here's a taste of classic mob-vernacular from the great film *Goodfellas* (1990):

```
                    HENRY (V.O.)
      Before you could touch a made
      guy, you had to have a good reason.
      There had to be a sit-down. And
      you better get an okay, or you'd be
      the one who got whacked.
```

"Made guy," "a sit-down," and "whacked" are just a few examples of what's become popular Mafia-esque vernacular. Even if you are unfamiliar with these terms and their word usages, you get a sense of what they mean. It's still fairly clear. It's interesting to note that the writers Martin Scorsese and Nicholas Pileggi were both very adept at understanding Mafia culture. Pileggi was a journalist, an author, and a screenwriter who was actually regarded as an expert on the Italian Mafia. In 1986, he wrote the book *Wiseguy*, which *Goodfellas* was based on. The point here is that for your characters to speak authoritatively, you need to supply them with authoritative and authentic-*sounding* dialogue to speak. Unless you are writing in a vernacular that you are confidently familiar with, do the work it takes to get it right. Getting it wrong can be fatal.

8

TOOL KIT – WRITING SINGULAR CHARACTERS

- Introduction: Tool kit – Writing singular characters
- Finding character
- Conflict
- Quirky and unique logic
- Energy: Passion and pop content

Introduction: Tool kit – Writing singular characters

We all strive to write singular characters, characters that are so vibrant and unique that they sear a hole into our minds and hearts. We carry them with us forever, sometimes even longer than we remember the stories that they inhabited. Although dialogue alone doesn't unto itself create a character in total, it certainly can hugely contribute to how we perceive and remember them. In screen narratives, as opposed to prose, characters are often defined by what they do. Their actions, literally what the audience sees them physically doing, is definitely a major component to who they are. But it is often a combination of what they do *and* what they say that makes them so compelling and memorable. When we think of John Travolta's character, Vincent, in *Pulp Fiction*, it isn't just the image of him thrusting a syringe into Uma Thurman's heart in order to save her, but also his banter. This includes his amazement that the Dutch eat their French fries with mayonnaise: "I seen 'em do it. And I don't mean a little bit on the side of the plate, they fuckin' drown 'em in it"

In this chapter, we're going to examine various qualities of singular characters and how their dialogue is a manifestation of who they are. In learning how to recognize that what a character says is also who a character is, we'll show you how to begin to find language that helps to reflect and define who your characters are in greater depth, through their dialogue. In previous chapters, we've discussed how dialogue is often the last part of the process of screen and television writing. Even though we will be discussing some hypothetical characters, it must be understood that even before you commence putting words into characters' mouths, that you have already given significant consideration to who each character is. Even if in the actual process of writing the dialogue for a character you discover things about them that you hadn't known before, character development still requires focused attention outside of the dialogue writing process. For the most part, you know what major actions they will take; you know the plot of their story. Given that you likely have at least a rudimentary understanding of your characters before you write their dialogue, we're going to also consider ways to raise the entertainment value along the way.

Finding character ·

When Clint Eastwood's character, "Dirty" Harry Callahan, says the famous catchphrase "Go ahead, make my day" in the film *Sudden Impact* (1983), it blends seamlessly into who his character is. In other words, memorable lines and famous catchphrases don't simply appear in a vacuum and randomly pop out of characters' mouths. They are brilliantly constructed products of both the dramatic context of the story, as well as the very essences of the characters that utter them. *Essences of the characters that utter them.*

When SFPD Homicide Inspector Dirty Harry says his famous line, it's early in the film, after it's been established that he's frustrated by the legal loopholes in San Francisco that have allowed violent criminals to go free. While at his favorite diner, he interrupts a robbery and kills three of the criminals. Then he targets the remaining bandit with his drawn .44 Magnum and challenges him to make a move, saying: "Go ahead, make my day." In so many ways, this line is the *essence* of who Harry is: a tough, hard-boiled cop with an acute sense of justice, seething with suppressed anger over a lifetime of inequities in a world where victims have little recourse and violent perpetrators run free. When he says "Go ahead, make my day," the sheer economy of the sentence succinctly expresses just how itching he is to blow this guy's head off, to make a dent in a world of injustice. It speaks to his deepest concerns and it informs his core belief system, his moral outrage. It also lets us know that he's chronically on a short fuse, capable of erupting at any moment. And with this line, we know who he is for the rest of the story.

* * *

The subject of character is vast and can take up many volumes. And although in a later chapter we will discuss methods to learn more about your characters, we will focus here on how characters' dialogues should be direct expressions of who they essentially are. Platitudes about what constitutes a strong character are endless, including:

Character is like a tree and reputation like a shadow. The shadow is what we think of it; the tree is the real thing. —Abraham Lincoln

And

The best index to a person's character is how he treats people who can't do him any good, and how he treats people who can't fight back. —Abigail Van Buren

And all of the platitudes have some truth to them. *But for our purposes here, understanding character as it determines and effects the dialogue they speak, it is good to keep in mind that your characters, like real people, are complex. And when we speak of complexities, we usually think about inner conflicts, hypocrisies, and inconsistencies.* Even if in film we might not always have the opportunities to illuminate complexities of character in as great a depth as say a novel, we should still recognize, or at least consider, such complexities in our characters.

It's easy to be drawn into the clichés of character types, such as the A-type, the victim, the caretaker, etc. And it might not be such a bad place to start. Consider familiarizing yourself with basic psychological concepts, especially in regard to character types and traits. Although there seems to be less of a consensus regarding actual types, there are five personality traits that are more widely accepted in mainstream psychology today: neuroticism, extraversion, openness, agreeableness, and conscientiousness. The dynamics of each trait are complex and there is an abundance of crossovers and hybrids per individual.

There are numerous and evolving theories and studies about personality. For example, the Myers-Briggs Type Indicator, inspired by the work of psychologist Carl Jung, has codified sixteen personality types, each with a set of traits. They are the "Logistician," the "Defender," the "Executive," the "Mediator," and twelve more. Some of the traits noted for the Mediator, for example, include being poetic, kind, altruistic, and eager to help a good cause. It's fairly logical to imagine how identifying some of these traits with a character might inspire their dialogue and their actions.

A good screenwriter is a constant student of behavior. *It might be helpful to make a list of character traits for each of your major characters.* And then see if you can imagine language that might be specific to some of those traits. Using the example of the Mediator type mentioned earlier, and her traits including being poetic, kind, altruistic, and eager to help a good cause, you can easily envision that this person might include in her pallet of ideas and thoughts words and terms such as "co-dependence," "non-profit," "Walt Whitman," "compassion," "empathy," "enabling." This list could also include an endless number of poets; poems; poetical language; and thoughts about fairness, balance, and justice.

Much of this is common sense and we automatically speak from the various traits that make us individuals. As you create dialogue for your characters, consider their traits and see if in doing so, new or additional words and ideas emerge.

Remember, you are *inventing* everything about your characters, both from the beginning and as you go along.

Conflict

If we agree that a major tenant of what is considered "drama" is conflict, and that dramatic writing is what constitutes compelling film and television scriptwriting, then it behooves you to not only be aware of when it occurs in scripted conversation, but also to learn how to replicate it in your own work. *This is especially true since your characters are more easily revealed through conflict than they are without it.* When we seriously examine even ordinary conversation, you might be surprised how much conflict weaves itself throughout it. Consider that conflict includes all manners of tension, resistance, obstacles, and problems. When you detect snideness in another's voice, or in your own, that is a subtle form of conflict. So is irony and sarcasm. Humor is filled with tension and conflict. Remember, it is comedic to see someone slip on a banana peel, but it's dramatic if we are the one slipping. But in either case, someone is falling, potentially injuring themselves, and yet we laugh. Humor is often at the expense of someone else. *Conflict.*

Even much of our enjoyable conversations are rife with conflict. We love to argue with each other over ideas and opinions. Arguing is full of tension. Even benign conversations between friends so often belies subtextual personal agendas that are antagonistic or covertly full of anger or upset. Honesty itself sometimes is the product of extreme tension and upset. One's resistance to telling the truth to another or admitting to oneself a truth can be excruciatingly tense and stressful, even between lovers.

Pain is conflict. It is stressful and it tugs against one's natural desire to be painless. Pain, and any form of uncomfortableness, or having one's feelings bruised, creates various levels of tension and conflict. Differing opinions and agendas, opposing ideas, even disagreeing on which restaurant to eat at, is conflict. Being alive is a tense affair. To write compelling dialogue, lean into it.

Two important benefits of conflict

There are two enormous benefits of conflict in scripted narratives: (1) Film and TV with conflict are considerably more watchable and compelling than without conflict. (2) Through conflict, characters often reveal who they are or deeper layers of themselves.

1. *Film and TV with conflict are considerably more watchable and compelling than without conflict.* There are neurological explanations having to do with evolutionary biology in regard to survival: Conflict triggers survival buttons. Just as neuroscience research has suggested that primate brains are hard-wired to detect snakes and spiders as threats to survival, likely for similar reasons,

"drama" is more compelling than no drama. And by compelling, let's be clear, we're talking about demanding attention from an audience.

2. *Through conflict, characters often reveal who they are or deeper layers of themselves.* As conflict tends to heighten emotions, the border between rational and less rational behavior equally tends to dissolve. Consequently, in this heightened state, people act and speak in uncensored ways that lay bare aspects of themselves that even they might not even be aware of.

Good writers of dialogue know this and go out of their way to find and create conflict. *Find and create.* A telling example is on page two of Rian Johnson's script *Knives Out* (2019). It's the first time that we meet Marta Cabrera, the caretaker of the deceased Harlan Thrombey and the lead character among an ensemble of characters. The scene is there for us to meet Marta in her humble home surroundings, in contrast to the opulent wealth of Harlan's world and the mansion she had worked in.

INT. CABRERA KITCHEN - MORNING

Marta sits in front of a laptop. Her MOM is at the table with her, her sister ALICE watches CSI on an iPad on the countertop. Murder related dialog from the show. Marta scrolls through a jobs site, tired, eyes dead. Her mom watches, concerned.

> MOM
> Alice, turn that off now.

> ALICE
> Why it's almost over, what - they're finding out who did it and the wifi sucks in my room so it doesn't play it's like two minutes left what there isn't even anything bad on it, it's just normal tv and they're just talking ok ok goddddd whatever ok whatever.

> MOM
> Now please just turn it off. Turn it off. Now. Alice. Off. They're talking about murder on it, your sister just had a friend she loves slit his throat open she doesn't need to be hearing that right now let's be sensitive!

Mom standing yelling, Alice slams the iPad cover
closed. Marta puts her head in her hand. Looks at her
mom, who looks back at her with protective sympathy.
Marta starts laughing at the absurdity of it, but the
laugh turns into crying.

                    MARTA
          Alice you can keep watching your show
          it's alright.

                    ALICE
          No, I guessed who did it anyway. I'm
          sorry Marta.

The purpose of this scene is for us to meet Marta in her ordinary, humble surroundings and know that she's a good person. It's important that we learn that
she has a loving, supportive relationship with her immigrant mother and sister,
everything that is the opposite of the wealthy family she works for. There are
any number of ways a writer could set this up without any overt tension. We
know that Marta's employer has recently died, but aside from sadness and perhaps even financial insecurity, there's no specific need or reason for additional
conflict. This is especially true if you want to show Marta as mentally stable
and loving, you might go out of your way to *not* include additional conflict.
But what's interesting is that Johnson purposely creates a loud, tense argument
between Marta's mother and sister. And though it is over a relatively petty
thing, through this argument we learn how much her mother and sister really
care for Marta, as well as how upset Marta is and how loving and sensitive they
all are toward each other. We also learn about their relative economic status as
it's revealed that their Wi-Fi works best only in the kitchen. This scene is all
the more watchable and compelling because of this conflict. It's full of passion
and raised voices.

   Johnson invented this argument and you can too. There are an infinite number of potential arguments lurking nearly everywhere you look. In this case, it's
as simple as the conflict of Marta's mother entreating her daughter to shut off
her internet program because she's sensitive to how the violent images might
affect Marta. But when you think about creating conflict this way, it is quite
easy to pick fights, invent arguments, and create conflict – even for the best
and most loving reasons. Imagine that Marta's sister was angry that her internet
wasn't working and got into an argument with her mother over that. Or that
Marta's mother was upset about unpaid utility bills, overuse of the internet, or
that Marta's sister argued about not wanting to wash her plate. The point is that
conflicts are everywhere.

   Think conflict. It's much easier for your character to react to conflicting situations than to just start talking. Reacting has more energy. You'll see that it is also
easier for them to speak more emotionally and honestly if they are compelled to

react. And in doing so, they reveal aspects of themselves that will help us know and identify with them.

Quirky and unique logic

Quirks – Unusual, peculiar and unexpected character traits or aspects that often tend to dominate a character's personality.

As it applies to dialogue, there can be (1) quirky characters whose language might be less unique, but whose dialogue content reflects their peculiarities; (2) quirky word choices and terms – odd, colorful words and terms – that emit from unique, quirky characters; or (3) fairly normal characters who use quirky and colorful language. Let's first look at an example of the first application.

Imagine this family: a misanthropic teenage boy with a mohawk who refuses to speak because of his recent infatuation with the philosophy of Friedrich Nietzsche; a subversive, heroin-snorting grandpa; a chubby little daughter who delusionally aspires to be a child beauty queen; a gay, suicidal, middle-aged unemployed Proust scholar uncle; a deeply insecure and unsuccessful self-help motivational-speaker father; and a guilty, exhausted, overworked smoking-addicted, mediator mother. On many levels, this is the definition of a quirky family. It's the family in the film *Little Miss Sunshine* (2006). As you can see by even their briefest descriptions, each character has specific quirks.

In an early scene around the dinner table, the conversation flows directly to and from each of their various quirks. And of equal importance, their logic, the way they think about the world, also presents itself. From the aforementioned character descriptions, it should be fairly easy to identify who each character is:

                    RICHARD
         It's been nine months. He hasn't
         said a word. I think it shows
         tremendous discipline.

                    SHERYL
         Richard...

                    RICHARD
         I'm serious! I think we could all
         learn something from what Dwayne's
         doing! Dwayne has a goal. He has a
         dream. It may not be my dream, or
         your dream, but still... He's pursuing
         that dream with focus and discipline.
         In fact, I was thinking about the
         Nine Steps...

                    GRANDPA
Oh, for crying out loud...!

                    RICHARD
                  (evenly)
...About the Nine Steps, and how
Dwayne's utilizing at least seven of
them in his journey to personal
fulfillment.

                    SHERYL
Richard. Please.

                    RICHARD
I'm just saying! I've come around! I
think Dwayne deserves our support.

Frank looks at Dwayne. Dwayne rolls his eyes. Olive
addresses Frank.

                    OLIVE
How did it happen?

                    FRANK
How did what happen?

                    OLIVE
Your accident...

                    SHERYL
Honey...

She shakes her head: "Don't go there."

                    FRANK
No, it's okay. Unless you object...

                    SHERYL
No, I'm pro-honesty here. I just
think, you know... It's up to you.

                    FRANK
Be my guest...

                    SHERYL
Olive, Uncle Frank didn't really
have an accident. What happened was:
he tried to kill himself.

                              OLIVE
          You did? Why?

                              RICHARD
          I don't think this is an appropriate
          conversation.
                    (to Olive)
          Let's leave Uncle Frank alone.

A beat. Olive has stopped eating.

                              OLIVE
          Why did you want to kill yourself?

                              RICHARD
          Frank. Don't answer that question.

Frank stares at Richard. He turns back to Olive.

                              FRANK
          I tried to kill myself because I was
          very unhappy.

                              RICHARD
                    (overlapping)
          Don't listen, honey, he's sick and
          he doesn't know what he's...

                              SHERYL
          Richard... Richard... Richard...

                              RICHARD
          What?! I don't think it's appropriate
          for a six year old!

                              SHERYL
          She's gonna find out anyway. Go on,
          Frank.

                              OLIVE
          Why were you unhappy?

Frank glances at Richard -- deadpan victorious -- and
continues.

                              FRANK
          Well, there were a lot of reasons.
          Mainly, though, I fell in love with
          someone who didn't love me back...

                    OLIVE
Who?

                    FRANK
One of my grad students. I was very
much in love with him.

                    OLIVE
Him? It was a boy? You fell in love
with a boy?

                    FRANK
Yes. I did. Very much so.

This is new to Olive. She thinks it over.

                    OLIVE
That's silly.

                    FRANK
You're right. It was very, very silly.

                    GRANDPA
There's another word for it...

                    RICHARD
Dad....

                    OLIVE
So... That's when you tried to kill
yourself...?

                    FRANK
Well, no. What happened was: the boy
I was in love with fell in love with
another man, Larry Sugarman.

                    SHERYL
Who's Larry Sugarman?

                    FRANK
Larry Sugarman is perhaps the second
most highly regarded Proust scholar
in the U.S.

                    RICHARD
Who's number one?

                    FRANK
That would be me, Rich.

                        OLIVE
        So... That's when you tried...?

                        FRANK
        Well, no. What happened was: I was a
        bit upset. I did some things I
        shouldn't have done. Subsequently, I
        was fired, forced to leave my
        apartment and move into a motel.

                        OLIVE
        Oh. So that's when...?

                        FRANK
                 (hesitates)
        Well, no. Actually, all that was
        okay. What happened was: two days
        ago the MacArthur Foundation decided
        to award a "genius" grant to Larry
        Sugarman.
                 (deep breath)
        And that's when...

                        GRANDPA
        ...You tried to check out early.

                        FRANK
        Yes. And I failed at that as well.

                        RICHARD
        Olive, what's important to understand
        is that Uncle Frank gave up on
        himself. He made a series of foolish
        choices, and then he gave up on
        himself, which is something that
        winners never do.

Not your run-of-the-mill dinner conversation, but when you have characters with huge, peculiar quirks that define their personalities, this kind of uniquely peculiar content of dialogue more easily finds its way out of their mouths. *Note*: What's important is not just *what* they are talking about, but *how* they are talking about things in ways that both reflect their quirks and traits, and also the way they think about the world, their logic. Frank is devastated and suicidal not only from being jilted romantically, but also from being jilted academically by not receiving the MacArthur "Genius Award." He is even aware of his own petty stupidity. This is the mind of a self-aware, insecure, and romantic academic with an oversized ego. Everything he says expresses these aspects.

Likewise, Richard is forever interjecting his self-help mentality. Olive is faithfully childish, naive, and genuinely curious. Throughout the entire scene, we also learn how Sheryl, the mother, and their son, Dwayne, also think about the world. This is a uniquely eccentric family sincerely speaking from their hearts, not particularly using stylized or outsized language, but the content of what they speak about is unto itself peculiar and less expected at your average family dinner.

The second type of quirky dialogue has more to do with peculiar, odd, and even bizarre word and term usage from equally singular and stylized characters. The following example, from *Juno* (2007), is a scene in which Juno's friend Leah is picking Juno up from the abortion clinic. *Note*: Even with stylized language we're still able to glimpse the logic of Juno, who is herself a stylized, if slightly eccentric, character.

LEAH

What are you doing here, dumbass? I
thought I was supposed to pick you
up at four.

JUNO

I couldn't do it, Leah! It smelled
like a dentist in there. They had
these really horrible magazines, with,
like, spritz cookie recipes and bad
fiction and water stains, like someone
read them in the tub. And the
receptionist tried to give me these
weird condoms that looked like
grape suckers, and she told me about
her boyfriend's pie balls, and
Su-Chin Kuah was there, and she told
me the baby had fingernails.
Fingernails!

LEAH

Oh, gruesome. I wonder if the baby's
claws could scratch your vag on the
way out?

We can see Juno's logic, even if it's not particularly "unique" in that many people might make a similar choice about keeping an unborn child. But what's oddly unique are the things that she focuses on in the process of her decision: "spritz cookie recipes and bad fiction and water stains, like someone read them in the tub," and "weird condoms that looked like grape suckers and she told me about her boyfriend's pie balls." And these curious words and terms help to define

Juno, the character, and the entire tone of the film. It also makes, for those who
love it, incredibly entertaining. *Note*: Quirky word usage can sometimes sound
forced and render the tone more stylized, alienating, than intended.

For quirky dialogue from otherwise "normal" teenage boys that amazingly
informs their unique logic while being incredibly amusing, let's look at a section
of the following scene from *Superbad* (2007). In this scene Evan and Seth are
examining the new fake ID card that Fogell just got.

                         EVAN
                  (reading the card)
            Okay Mr..."McLovin"? What kind of
            a stupid name is that? What are you
            trying to be, an Irish R&B singer?

                         FOGELL
            Well, they let you pick any name you
            want when you get there.

                         SETH
            So you picked McLovin?

                         FOGELL
            It was between that or Muhammad.

                         SETH
            Why was it between that or Muhammad?
            Why didn't you just pick a common
            name?

                         FOGELL
            Actually, Seth, Muhammad is the most
            commonly used name on earth.

                         EVAN
            Have you ever actually met a guy
            named Muhammad?

                         FOGELL
            Have you actually ever met a guy
            named McLovin?

                         SETH
            No! That's why you picked a bad name.

                         EVAN
            You probably have federal agents
            tracking you for even considering
            the name Muhammad on a fake ID!

                        SETH
Look at this shit man, you don't even
have a first name. It just says
"NAME: MCLOVIN"

                        EVAN
One name?

                        FOGELL
I just thought McLovin sounded old,
and the chicks would dig it.

                        EVAN
Under what circumstances would you
ever have to show a chick your ID?

                        FOGELL
She could ask. Or, I could just
show it to her.

                        SETH
Holy shit! I don't believe this.
This says you're fucking 25! Why
didn't you just put 21?

                        FOGELL
I knew you would ask that. Look, every
day, dozens of kids roll into the
liquor store with fake ID's trying to
act like Joe Casual. Each and every
one of these kids just so happens to
be 21 years old. Just how many 21
year-olds do you think there are?

                        SETH
Fool!

                        EVAN
Calm down! It's not terrible! This
might work, but it's up to you, Fogell.
They'll either think, "Oh, it's another
punk kid with a fake ID." Or, "Look,
it's McLovin, the twenty five year-old
organ donor". What's it gonna be?
Fogell takes a deep breath.

                        FOGELL
I am McLovin.

                              SETH
          You're not McLovin. No one's McLovin
          and this is never going to work. We
          need a new way to get alcohol. Could
          we drive to Canada or something?

                             FOGELL
          I still think it's going to work.

We know and love these boys. They are not particularly unusual or unique. Their language suggests that they are not "stupid," but rather quite intelligent and yet, still amazingly dumb in a sweet teenage boy kind of way. They are simply desperate teenagers craving to buy booze for all sorts of reasons we glean throughout the film. They know about how common the name Muhammad is, they speak of organ donors, they are quite self-aware, and yet one of them has come up with the preposterous single name "McLovin" for his fake ID. We see, and intuitively even understand, Fogell's delusional logic and sense of self. Similarly, we comprehend the logic of his friends' obvious frustration, yet desperate willingness to try anything. This is a scene in which otherwise normal kids distinguish themselves through their dialogue, and in doing so, moves the story forward, widens our understanding of their characters, and entertains us in the best of ways.

Energy: Passion and pop content

When we think about the dialogue we love, the one commonality is the energy we *feel* from the characters. A huge aspect of this energy is their *passion*. In so many of the examples we have looked at so far, whether it's teenagers in *Juno* and *Superbad*, hitmen in *Pulp Fiction*, heroin addicts in *Trainspotting*, suburbanites in *Little Miss Sunshine* and *American Beauty*, or all the period dramas, urban street, college and police narratives, passion reigns supreme.

So, what are we talking about when we speak of a character's passion or a passionate character? A strong appetite, particular partiality and preference, relish, craving, desire, infatuation, intensity, longing, lust, yearning, ardor, eagerness, enthusiasm, fervor, devotion and zeal. Put all these together and a good working definition is the first definition that pops up in a Google search: *A strong and barely controllable emotion*. Strong *and* barely controllable.

Not every single character displays this sort of passion every time they open their mouths. Remember, it takes energy simply to speak. When you're too tired to speak, you don't. But we are here because of dialogue and characters who do speak. Even if they physically cannot speak because of a disability, we still may hear in voice-over their inner thoughts that are full of energy and passion. The following is a snippet from the Academy Award–winning short film *Stutterer* (2015), in which the main character, Greenwood, has a severe speech impediment. We only hear his dialogue as a stream-of-consciousness voice-over.

```
              GREENWOOD
Snap judgment 1225. Charity worker.
Dependable. Funny, the choir and large
groups...dreams of escaping, to born
his errors, to set up a wine bar,
laughs words, and despises his
text-speak.
```

It is perfectly clear that Greenwood is highly intelligent, very articulate, and bristling with a passion to communicate. We can also see that his struggle with communication is what his story is about. It's also what makes him memorable and unique. Characters that have energetic dialogue are usually passionate about something, and that something is either related to their goals, wants, needs, or inner goals, or they are evoked through conflict. And since conflict, as we've learned, often cues a subliminal threat to survival, we can see how characters can easily become passionate when they sense that their survival is at stake, even if it is survival of pride, ego, or saving face.

Previously, we've discussed the importance of specificity in word and term usage. I want to point out how using very specific pop references in particular tend to inform a certain passion in our characters. Whether it's evoking "Big Mac and fries," "Blair Witch on Starz," or "text-speak," when characters snatch pop terms from the zeitgeist of cultural babble that they inhabit, it creates sparks of energy. Even if we as an audience are unfamiliar with the references or the time period, it gives characters added authority. That alone evokes energy and passion.

Memorable dialogue flows from characters who are connected, though often unconsciously, with their passions, even if they are depressed, uncharismatic, or incapacitated. Strive to find the uniqueness of your characters, and in that process, you will also begin to find their singular voices, their unique words, and the ways that they say them. And as you hone their uniqueness, you will inevitably begin to unleash their essential life force, or singular energy. With conflict and energy, your characters will take on a life of their own. Their passions will emerge. You are the puppeteer of your characters and you can make them dance, and speak, as energetically and as passionately as you want.

9

TOOL KIT – NATURALISTIC DIALOGUE, THEMES, AND EXPOSITION PROBLEMS

- Introduction: Tool kit – Naturalistic dialogue, themes, and exposition problems
- Naturalistic dialogue
- Themes
- Remedying exposition

Introduction: Tool kit – Naturalistic dialogue, themes, and exposition problems

By this point, it should be clear that replicating normal, everyday conversation is not what makes strong scripted dialogue. We've established how real conversations are typically boring, off point, and, if efficient in some respects, not particularly entertaining – nor should it be. In real life, we communicate for all sorts of reasons, and most of the reasons aren't absolutely necessary. They often serve simple, human, and emotional needs. Try to not communicate for an afternoon at home if you live with others and notice how essential communication is; so much of our talking to one another comes from our habit of interacting and sharing. We don't want to feel lonely. What we say and talk about is fairly pointless in terms of the narratives of our lives: "How are you," "Look at this," "What's going on?" etc. As discussed earlier, our scripted stories are also not simply slices of uneventful living. They are heightened, hopefully interesting, and they aspire to be compelling. Still, there are aspects of real life and real conversations that we can use toward consciously creating certain effects. When we speak of *naturalistic dialogue*, we are specifically thinking about the tics, rhythms, cadences, and other precise sonic aspects of how people actually speak. This also includes how those elements can be conveyed on the page and to what effect.

We will also look at how understanding the themes and underlying ideas of your scripts can guide you to a host of various word and language usages in your dialogue.

Finally, the problems of exposition plague many writers: How do you get what you consider essential information to an audience or other characters while sounding natural?

Naturalistic dialogue

When we think about ultra real-sounding characters, who comes to mind? Larry David's characters on *Curb Your Enthusiasm* (2000)? Joe Swanberg's characters in his series *Easy* (2016)? The characters in the *Before* trilogy (*Before Sunrise, Before Sunset, Before Midnight*)? Although "improving" will be covered in a later chapter, the vast majority of *Curb Your Enthusiasm*'s dialogue is invented and spoken spontaneously and improvisationally; it is not scripted.

In a certain respect, conversations without verbal tics, the "ums" and the "ahs," might be the equivalent of scripted drama without the humdrum, realistically boring parts. Or, like when you watch a nature documentary on leopards, it's nearly impossible to viscerally convey that the vast majority of the time that leopards just lie around without it being mind-numbingly boring. What we see is the tiny amount of action in their lives, when they hunt or mate. These are active, visual events. But what about the rest of the time? What about the "ums" and "ahs" that make up and take up a lot of the time and space of realistic conversation?

Whether you strive for dialogue that sounds absolutely pitch-perfect or not, it should still be purposeful, not boring, and should not take up unnecessary real estate. It's a known trick among journalists that if they perfectly replicate their interview subjects word-for-word they can spin it so they appear awkward and stupid. The main purpose of replicating exact aspects of language on the page would be to better articulate a character's personality and to give actors those precise idiosyncratic mannerisms of speech to help them create singular characters. Woody Allen has nearly pioneered the path of literally writing out dialogue in a naturalistic way, with all the verbal tics included. In doing so he's able to conjure the nuanced neurosis of his characters. Read (and listen to) this excerpt, from *Annie Hall* (1977):

```
                    ANNIE
        Alvy, I ...

                    ALVY
        What-what-what-what's the matter?

                    ANNIE
        I-you know, I don't wanna.
```

```
                    ALVY
        (Overlapping Annie, reacting)
    What-what-I don't ... It's not natural!
    We're sleeping in a bed together. You
    know, it's been a long time.


                   ANNIE
    I know, well, it's just that-you know,
    I mean, I-I-I-I gotta sing tomorrow
    night, so I have to rest my voice.
```

Or this excerpt from Noah Baumbach's *Marriage Story* (2019):

```
                   NICOLE
    I want a...I don't know, I'm trying to
    say this as undramatically as possible.
    I want an ENTIRELY different kind of life.
```

Or this from *Girls* (2012), written by Lena Dunham:

```
                  HANNAH
    No, now. I need you to read them
    now. Because... I feel like I've
    been hiding something from you.
        (pause)
    I don't want to freak you out,
    but...
        (pause)
    I think I may be the voice of my
    generation.
        (pause)
    At least a voice. A strong voice.
```

- *Let commas, capitalizing, question marks, exclamation points, (pauses), em dashes, and ellipses help you finely articulate singular, precisely mannered dialogue, and sounds and verbal tics.* Example: sllurrring, stu-stut-stuttering, lithping, or mummberbling. And in the process, you can convey the nuanced, complex manner in which your character's mind works.
- Real people pause, interrupt, stutter, speak in fragments, say random things/thoughts, talk over each other, don't acknowledge, don't complete their sentences, repeat themselves, and wander off.
- Real language is full of "ums," "uhs" and "whatchamacallits," etc., as place holders for gaps in thinking or lapses in memory.
- People sometimes say the wrong word by accident or through a misunderstanding of its meaning.

Themes

The theme of a story is the underlying idea(s) and concepts that, like DNA, wind their way into the very fiber of the entire narrative. It's what a story is essentially about, not plot or event-wise, but the very underlying notions that animate the narrative. Other than the entire story itself, dialogue is a significant vehicle to illuminate the screenplay's themes. They might appear as direct ideas that literally articulate the themes ("Get busy livin' or get busy dyin'" – *The Shawshank Redemption*). They might be revealed obliquely, dotting conversations throughout the whole story.

You can hardly think of a single significant scene of *The Godfather* (1972) that doesn't speak to the complexity of family dynamics. If the major theme of *The Godfather* is the *complexity of family dynamics*, you might list loyalty, honor, and patriarchy as possible subthemes. But family dynamics is the primary theme. You can speak about the themes of your story without ever mentioning the plot of the story itself. Similarly, you can talk about the themes of *The Godfather* without ever mentioning the Italian Mafia, etc. The ideas and concepts regarding the complexity of family dynamics inform and shape the characters and the story. Identifying and prioritizing what you believe are the prominent themes of your script can help you find poignant content for your characters to talk about. It can also potentially give you a host of words, language, and concepts to weave into your dialogue.

Identifying themes can fundamentally help a writer find important scenes, which would then obviously bleed into the dialogue. Continuing to use *The Godfather* as an example, the following are a few snippets of dialogue that illustrate how the theme of the complexity of family dynamics is innate to what's spoken. And for those who have seen the film, they clearly appear and inform nearly every pivotal scene of the film:

"The only wealth in this world is children. More than all the money, power on Earth, you are my treasure."

"Tell me. Do you spend time with your family?" "Good. Because a man who doesn't spend time with his family can never be a real man."

"Fredo, you're my older brother, and I love you. But don't take sides against the family again. Ever."

"I don't want anything to happen to him while my mother's alive."

"I, uh, betrayed my wife. I betrayed myself. I've killed men, and I've ordered men to be killed. No, it's useless. I killed ... I ordered the death of my brother; he injured me. I killed my mother's son. I killed my father's son."

"Oh, Michael, Michael, you are blind. It wasn't a miscarriage. It was an abortion, Michael. Just like our marriage is an abortion, something that's unholy and evil. I didn't want your son, Michael."

"I swear on the lives of my children. Give me one last chance to redeem myself, and I will sin no more."

The theme of *family dynamics* is certainly not limited to *The Godfather*. It's one of the major themes in all of literature, drama, and film. Whether it is prominent in a gangster tale, a comedy, a struggling parent or child story, or a drama of addiction, many of the same issues, and therefore dialogue, will appear. The dialogue will clearly have to be recalibrated to fit the specific characters, but whether the character is a junkie or a psychiatrist, if they are dealing with family issues as the primary theme, a reasonable amount of their thinking and speaking will concern these issues. Trust, loyalty, betrayal, fear, and abandonment are just the tip of the iceberg when it comes to family dynamics. If you make a list of these words and synonyms that might be appropriate for your different characters, you can widen your palate of vocabulary and concepts to pepper throughout your dialogue. Suddenly, the notion of *trust* might inspire language that could include "you're not reliable," "how can I believe you or myself?" "tell me the truth," "what we had between us is broken," "give it to me straight," "how do I know you'll stay?" "you need to prove it to me," "you were never there," and so on.

Similarly, if the primary theme is *redemption*, which is also a common theme, we can again think about synonyms and related concepts that might include forgiveness, vindication, rescue, saving, help, fines, forgiving, redemption, healing, atonement, letting go, self-loathing, revelation, and honesty. For example, if we look at the dialogue in the film *The Fisher King* (1991), in which the primary theme is redemption, we can find snippets informed by this theme, its synonyms, and related concepts.

                    JACK (O.S.)
          Edwin... Edwin... Edwin... I told you
          about these people. They only mate
          with their own kind. It's called
          Yuppie-In-Breeding... that's why so
          many of them are retarded and wear
          the same clothes. They're not human.
          They can't feel love. They can only
          negotiate love moments. They're
          evil, Edwin. They're repulsed by

imperfection and horrified by the
banal -- everything America stands
for. Edwin, they have to be stopped
before it's too late. It's us or
them.

                    ***

                    JACK
          "Hey...for-...

False start. JACK clears his throat, pauses, then
tries again...

                    JACK
               (sarcastic...insincere...)
          "Hey! Forgiiiive ME!"

CUT TO;

JACK'S BEDROOM - NIGHT.

Alarm clock reads 11:15. JACK is still rehearsing,
while the T.V. plays with no sound.

                    JACK
          " HEY! Forgive MEEE!" ...
          ...FOR-GIVE-ME ...
          Hey...forgive me!
               (HE smiles and shuts the script:)
          I have this...I really have this...

                    ***

                    JACK
          I wish there was some way I could...
          just... pay the fine and go home.

                    ***

                    JACK
          I'm self-centered, I'm weak - I don't
          have the willpower of a fly on shit...

                    ***

                    PARRY
        ɔegin with the story itself.
        y of the Grail myth...And
        ıere are several variations,
        e begins with the Fisher King
        ɟ boy... who had to spend a
        ıe in the forest to prove his
        . and during that night, he
        ᵊd by a sacred vision. Out of
        _   appears the Holy Grail - God's
highest symbol of divine grace. And a
voice says to the boy, "You shall be the
guardian of the Grail, that it may heal
the hearts of men."

                    ***

                    PARRY
But I need help and they sent you.

                    ***

                    PARRY
        (continuing)
I was married. I was married to this
beautiful woman.... And you were there
too...
                (pause)
I really miss her, Jack. Is that
okay? Can I miss her now?

The takeaway here is that knowing your themes can be another tool in your tool
kit for raising the quality and tone of your dialogue.

   Here is a checklist to help you in your process:

- Identify your themes.
- Prioritize them.
- List synonyms for them and related concepts they inspire that would fit your
  story and your characters.
- Imagine your characters speaking these words, thinking about, and/or being
  informed by these terms, concepts, and themes in direct, obscure, and inadvertent ways.
- Envision how your themes and related concepts might suggest scenes and
  situations – and dialogue by the characters in the scenes and situations.

Remedying exposition

Lorenzo Semple Jr., the screenwriter of *Three Days of the Condor* (1975), *Parallax View* (1974), and many other big Hollywood films of the '70s once said to me, "If you want your characters to say any exposition, have 'em say it while they're dangling from a rope."

Exposition simply means information that an audience needs to know to contextualize and understand the story. Dialogue is a great way to convey expository information.

Typically, exposition is information about a character or the situation at hand that is given to the audience in order for the rest of the story to have the maximum impact and meaning. Often, this includes information from the past, including events from before the story that we're watching takes place. But sometimes, because the characters already know what has occurred, it's unnatural for them to spell it out to each other. Yet it is important for the audience to know. Or so you think.

If exposition is information that you feel is important for a character, the audience, or both to know, then the first thing to ask is, *How important is it that it must be expressed now?* We're writers, so we write. Oftentimes we write too much. In the terrific indie film *Leave No Trace* (2018), a fair amount of the dialogue in the script was ultimately not spoken because, through the amazing performance of Ben Foster, it was considered unnecessary. Writers write, but sometimes forget just how powerful and communicative expressions and performances are. Ingmar Bergman allegedly said that what separates films from plays is the close-up of the face. This goes doubly for expository information. So often what you think is absolutely necessary is either not needed at all or not needed when you think it is. Mystery and oblique or incomplete information is a basic tool of all good storytelling. It makes the audience want to continue watching.

- **The problems**

  For screen and TV writers the problems of exposition typically are:

  1. You either find yourself squeezing information into dialogue that feels unnatural or cluttered. It's clearly intended for the audience to hear and less for the other characters.
  2. You want a character or the audience to know some information and you suddenly add it as a non sequitur. It's that sudden jump to another subject that you add because you believe it's essential for the characters, the audience, or both to know.
  3. You want the audience to know something, but the characters obviously already know that information. A corollary to this is you have characters discussing something that they would have already previously covered. For example, two characters jump in a car and zoom off. Then you CUT to them getting out of their car, having arrived at their destination, and they talk about things that, logically, they would have already talked about in the car on their way there. Similarly, a couple

married for many years wouldn't tell each other obvious details about their lives, since they would have already shared that information with each other.

- **The remedies**

The first and most important step toward remedying these problems is to identify them. This can be especially difficult for new writers, because they've already made their dialogue work in their mind's ear. They cannot detect it sounding unnatural, cluttered, obvious, or awkward.

1. *It often takes hearing your script read aloud by another person.* Ideally, this is done by an actor. But anyone, including yourself, will suffice. Do not hesitate to read your dialogue out loud to yourself. You'll be surprised by what you will hear.

This is especially useful for discerning cluttered, stilted, or awkward exposition. In the case of too much information or data, *slim it down and parse out the essential information through more back-and-forth exchanges between characters.* Make every effort to limit the information. But first, really question whether it is *that* important for the audience to know.

In terms of non sequitur information suddenly sounding awkward and unnatural, it just needs to be finessed. Sometimes people actually do radically change subjects. This often happens because the topic that people suddenly switch to is actually the main thing that they have been itching to talk about all along. But if you've identified an unnatural and sudden non sequitur, then consider having one of the characters, including the speaker, comment on it. For example, "Wow, where did that come from?" Or create a sufficient pause to indicate that the person has regrouped his thoughts.

2. Identifying the problem of whether the characters would have already known the information can also be tricky to discern. *It is a matter of first playing out the logic in your mind*, of both the contents of the dialogue as well as the timing, as in when it's spoken within the timeline of the script.

Once you've identified the information that would have been obviously self-evident, then you can remedy it by having the information restated in a variety of different ways. These include describing it in the directions; hearing the information as voice-over; having the information arise from a character answering a question; hearing it from a character telling a story, dream, or recollection; having another character who doesn't know the information enter the scene so it would be logical to say; or creating characters who would logically need to hear information, such as police officers, judges, psychologists, doctors, lawyers, parole officers, border guards, DMV clerks, new colleagues, or anyone new.

3. List the information that you feel is essential to be conveyed.

When you begin to write a scene, first record "your list of things that you want to convey to the audience." Here is an example scenario: (a) You want to convey that the characters are attending a college screenwriting class (b) that it is taking place at Columbia University. (c) The professor's nickname was Lucky. (d) The professor has won an Academy Award for a famous film that he wrote, which every student there would have known about. In this situation, you would not have the professor say:

> PROFESSOR JONES
> Hi everyone, it's good to see that you're
> all here in our classroom studying
> screenwriting at Columbia University. As
> you know, my nickname was "Lucky," although
> that's not what they called me when I won
> the Academy Award for Best Screenplay.

Remember that almost everything above would have already been known and obvious to all the students, except perhaps the nickname. You can convey this information much more naturally in a number of ways. For example, using the script directions, you can indicate that a student is wearing a Columbia sweatshirt. And by interacting with students, all of the already aforementioned information, as well as new info about the professor, can more seamlessly be revealed:

INT. COLLEGE CLASSROOM - DAY

PROFESSOR JONES (52) turns from the white board full of script diagrams toward TEN STUDENTS seated around a seminar table.

> PROFESSOR JONES
> ...at what point in the script should
> we know what the setup is?

STUDENT ONE, wearing a Columbia University sweatshirt, raises her hand and speaks.

> STUDENT ONE
> ...By the end of Act One?

> PROFESSOR JONES
> Okay, good.

> STUDENT TWO
> But Professor Jones, that's not how
> you did it in *The Graduate*.

> PROFESSOR JONES
> When I wrote that, I didn't know what
> I was doing.

```
                    STUDENT THREE
          It still won an Oscar.

                    PROFESSOR JONES
          FYI, my mom used to call me "Lucky."
          That's all I was with that script.
```

We've learned everything on the list of "things to be conveyed" in the scene. Use the script directions when possible. If it doesn't need to be said and you can *show it,* then that's the way to go. By turning the monologue into a conversation, it opens up the possibilities. Then it's about creating credible reasons or situations why characters would reveal information to us that they already know.

PART THREE

Exercises for better hearing and voicing your characters

Part Three explores methods, exercises, and applications for actually writing and improving your dialogue. Like any art form, proficiency requires devotion and maintenance. Similar to being a musician, writing dialogue competently takes both practice and listening. Learning *how* and *what* to listen to is key. This final section covers techniques and exercises to help *listen* to dialogue in a more beneficial manner. It also offers approaches to help connect with your characters' voices, as well as your own. Implementing routines and exercises is part of the ongoing process of writing in general, and dialogue writing is no exception. The idea is to apply what we've covered so far toward raising ordinary communication into entertaining and powerful dialogue. Implementing new habits, routines, and exercises regarding hearing and writing dialogue is an essential part of the ongoing screenwriting process.

10

ACCESSING CHARACTER
AND APPLICATION

Introduction: Accessing character and application

Where to start? What to do? Finally, here we are at the final part, Part Three, discussing the application of writing dialogue. The end is the logical place to begin, because now we have some ideas about what is needed and required. As previously covered, writing the dialogue is typically the frosting on the cake. There's so much you've already done, so much thinking about your stories and characters, your plot, structure, and themes. Because understanding your characters is as essential as understanding your story when writing good dialogue, and since this book concentrates less on narrative, we'll focus on some approaches for learning more about your characters.

There are many truths about a subject. Some seem to contradict each other. You'll hear about the writer who just sat down without any planning and cranked it out perfectly. You'll hear about another writer who just sat down, started with dialogue, and then "found" the whole story. There is a temptation to rush into it, to just start writing without much planning at all. Some people convince themselves that jumping into it is how they'll keep it fresh and spontaneous. Others just can't resist finding their way in the dark, one step at a time, not knowing where they're going and who their characters are. Whatever reasons people give, writing the script and the dialogue, whether it's good or not, *feels* easier than doing the prework.

Some people tell themselves that they just need to crank something out, then go back and clean it up, revise it, and make it better later. And maybe they will. But, especially for new writers, once they are sitting on a chunk of "finished" pages in scripted format, it's harder than ever to see the forest through the trees. And the "revisions" and the "clean-ups" that they envisioned doing later never happens, or become an overwhelming mess trying to fix the basic bones and architecture. And this goes double for attempting to fix a major character who, through her actions and words, is simply not working. Even without "natural dialogue-writing talent," you can still learn what is required to service the needs of your characters and raise the level of the dialogue that you write. Assuming you have a story, let's focus on how to start writing dialogue and understand your characters. Dialogue that is grounded in your character's inner life becomes more resonant, interesting, and compelling.

Character complexity

There's no single way to imagine your characters, no set rules or maps. You envision a character in your mind … and then suddenly, you might change her gender. His age. Her physique. Why? You're not sure, but you're trying to fit what you imagine into the whole. You want it to be authentic, but you also want it to be entertaining. You struggle for it to be both. You imagine your characters in different ways and once you make a change, your mind instantly attempts to fill in the blanks of everything else about the character that would need to change with it. Although theoretically anyone can say anything, we like characters who we believe. They can surprise us in behavior and dialogue, but we just need to feel like we know them enough for us to roll with any surprise, so that it feels deserved, earned, and organic.

Human beings are intrinsically complex. The novelist and educator John Gardner said:

> The writer's characters must stand before us with a wonderful clarity, such continuous clarity that nothing they do strike us as improbable behavior for just that character, even when the character's action is, as sometimes happens, something that came as a surprise to the writer himself. We must understand, and the writer before us must understand, more than we know about the character; otherwise neither the writer nor the reader after him could feel confident of the character's behavior when the character acts freely.

Obviously, this applies to film and television writing as well. Since, as has been covered, *character* is revealed by what a character does or says, dialogue is a prime vehicle for expressing and discovering a character's complexity.

Here are some classic elements of character complexity:

- *Contradiction.* Including beliefs, actions, morals, ideas, hypocrisies, and biases.
- *Internal conflict.* Of any kind. "I must, I can't," "I'm hot, I'm cold," "I'm pretty, I'm ugly," "I believe in God, I don't believe in God."
- *Inconsistencies.* We think we know someone by their routines, which certainly provide a snapshot of a character's ordinary life. But it's their inconsistencies that shed light on their individuality.
- *A variance of moods and emotions.* One does not have to be clinically bipolar in order to experience mental and emotional shifts. And this includes extreme emotions.
- *A singular adamant perspective.* This encompasses particularly unique or odd takes on a subject(s) as well as a hard fast traditional belief or dogma. Even if a character's belief is shifting and full of doubt, their particular slant or combination of traits can still make up a unique, singular, and adamant perspective.

Try to imagine conversations that emanate from, or are inspired by, the listed elements of complexity. Perhaps it is a political rant or an unwittingly self-contradicting statement. Maybe over the course of the story, a character's dialogue expresses opposite opinions and with various degrees of passion. It's endless, but by focusing on the complexities of your characters, with these and other characteristics in mind, let your imagination run loose and listen to them speak.

Character bios for dialogue

Following is a Biography Check Sheet that can help you know your major characters, or at least a preliminary version of them. It doesn't have to be completed in full for each character, although it might be a good start. Sometimes, as you write, characters will reveal themselves in a different way than how you envisioned them. Or you get a new idea about your character based on observing someone in your life, someone who you've seen in a film, or someone you read about in a book. If this happens, consider going with the change. Augment their biographies. Nothing is fixed. While writing drafts of your script, your Character Check Sheet will constantly evolve.

Character Check Sheet

As you answer the following questions, consider the range of conversations that each aspect listed might evoke.

Regarding your character:

- *What is their age?* This will certainly influence how and what they communicate. But, by putting adult words in adolescent characters or having seniors break out in rap can reveal unique characteristics and be entertaining.

- *What is their general intelligence level?* Someone can seem less formally intelligent but possess acute wisdom. Someone can be brilliant, but with a low emotional IQ.
- *Where are they from? Where were they raised?* This can affect their accents and the specific words and terms they use.
- *How were they raised?* Single parent? Multiple stepparents? Kind parents? Abusive? Although there is no absolute correlation between how a person was nurtured and how they will evolve, there is ample evidence about its importance. Knowing this about a character could shed light on her attitudes and beliefs.
- *What is their educational background?* School-smart? Self-taught? This might inform a variety of otherwise surprising words, concepts, and interests that your characters might speak about.
- *What is their physicality?* Are they disabled? Are they coordinated? Healthy? We can imagine a skinny person might have calories on their mind and want to talk about food.
- *What is their outer goal within your story?* What do they want to accomplish by the story's conclusion? Depending on how single-minded a character is, or how great the stakes are, they can have any aspects of their goal on the tip of their tongue.
- *What is their inner goal?* What unconsciously, or less consciously, motivates them to achieve their outer goal? This is where your subtext lives. A character whose goal is to win her bicycle race might have an unconscious inner goal to please her mom. It is this inner goal that motivates her to work so hard in order to win the race. All aspects of her relationship with her mom might then inform many subjects that she thinks about, and thus, talks about. This might even include her sense of victimhood, anger, or desperation.
- *What are their aspirations and secret aspirations?* A character might aspire to sing in his school musical and to be a famous rock star. Aspirations are always with you, and that includes the bitterness of failed aspirations. Aspirations tend to lead someone's interests, hobbies, and choices. They fill up a character's imagination and often want to be expressed.
- *What are their default moods?* What are their social moods? Their emotional types? Some characters are socially "happy," yet chronically depressed. Overcompensating suggests a kind of manic language. Some characters are quiet types, but have great personal agency and speak very few words.
- *What have they been doing over the last year?* Sketch out a brief outline of what they have been doing, where they've been living, and their relationships.
- *What are their highest moments and lowest moments before the story that they are in ever began?* So often in life, a particularly traumatic event can color everything that comes after it. It can inform choices, fears, and insecurities. It can also, either directly or indirectly, influence what a character might want to avoid talking about. Conversely, sometimes an amazingly wonderful time

or event takes on mythic proportions, even if unrealistically so. This too can inform the tone and content of a character's conversation, obsessions, and interests.

Application: What to do

So now you've done your prework, whatever that might mean to you. It's now time to write down what your characters are going to say to each other or to the audience. You envision your characters within the scene. You imagine their surroundings. Why are they there? Let's assume that you understand their purpose in the story at this point. There's a good chance that you are working on a scene that is designed to establish some information, push the story forward, reveal something about a character, or simply be entertaining. Often at the beginning of screen stories, one wants to establish the normal, ordinary universe that the characters inhabit. Sometimes this is before any catalytic event occurs that might set the story in motion.

What do your characters say? Imagine yourself in a similar position as your characters. You wonder what you might say in that situation. You draw a blank. Consider remembering something that you, the writer, has recently seen, read, or heard that might be worthy of telling your friends and family. What if one of your characters said it? How about, "Did you know that children of identical twins are genetically siblings, not cousins?" That might be an interesting conversation starter. Where did I get that odd bit of information? I Googled "weird facts." You can too.

Not every character would repeat that peculiar fact about sibling genetics. Not every character would have come across such information, and if they did, it wouldn't particularly make an impression. But try to imagine that dialogue in the mouths of your different characters. It's like trying on different clothes: What works? What fits? What looks good? What image does it affect? It's harder to imagine a grizzled, tough biker talking about sibling genetics than it is a precocious nerdy teen. But if that tough biker did say that information, it would certainly add an entirely new and surprising dimension to that character. Suddenly, in order to make it credible, you'd have to construct a new biography that would encompass this character's ability to come across and want to repeat this weird fact. Maybe he was more educated than you had previously imagined. Or he's a brilliant autodidact. Or he was raised in an orphanage by a geneticist nun. Somehow, it's justified. And now this trope of the hard-knuckled biker has expanded into a far more complex human being.

Five sources

There are five sources from where dialogue can come, and none of them are exclusive to each other. Although in Chapters Eleven and Twelve some of these sources are explored more thoroughly, for now understand that you can have any or all of these sources at your disposal. There is a great deal of overlap between them:

- *Your basic voice.* With your own voice and your own logic, write out the basic dialogue that you sense is essential to tell your story. One character says one thing and another responds or doesn't. It's how you would speak in that situation.
- *Character channeling.* You feel you know your characters enough to inhabit them. Write the dialogue as if the character is telling you what to say. (See "Character Channeling: Other voices" in Chapter Twelve.)
- *Mimicking.* Using an already-existing character's voice (usually from another film or novel), write your own character's dialogue. (See "Character Channeling: Mimicking" in Chapter Twelve.)
- *Collected dialogue.* Found, borrowed, stolen. or overheard. Pepper your dialogue with words or snippets of choice dialogue that you've collected. (See "Collecting Dialogue" in Chapter Eleven.)
- *Rewriting/revision.* Adding and changing what you have already written. Here you're striving for unique language, content, and sound. The key is to make your dialogue as compelling, revealing, and entertaining as possible. During this rewriting/revision process you might change what your characters say textually to subtextually. (See "Hearing and Improving Your Own Voice" in Chapter Twelve.)

What to do

Of course there are no absolute rules for writing dialogue. But here's a typically logical order on how to get started. Ready, get set, go:

- Envision the physical surrounding of your characters.
- Do they need to express some vital information at this moment? Is the scene there in order to push the story forward? Is it there to reveal something new about a character? Is it there simply because it's entertaining? Each of these reasons is not exclusive to the others. All four can be accomplished concurrently.
- Draw on your own imagination or memory for unique and memorable information that you've heard, read about, or invented. It might be an odd fact, rumor, or even a joke. Imagine your character saying it as you write it down.
- Google and research the kinds of information that your particular character might say or be interested in. Then write it down.
- Try out thoughts, ideas, and words that your character might *ordinarily not* talk about. Does it expand our understanding of that character? Does it give

your character greater depth? Maybe it doesn't fit. Maybe it ▓▓
on your character that you didn't even know before you wrote ▓

- Try out thoughts, ideas, and words that your character might *ordin* ▓
  about.
- Write the dialogue in your own speaking voice, if you do not yet hear your
  character's voice.
- Write your dialogue in the present tense. Allow us to experience what a
  character is feeling in the moment rather than her telling us. Instead of
  a character proclaiming that she feels physically bad, she might speak in
  strained, curt sentences that she's fine while she winces in agony. But, since
  there are no rules, she might simply say "I feel like shit!"
- How do you imagine your characters' lives before this moment, before they
  speak? Would their previous life experience inform what they might speak
  about at this moment?
- Does what they say fit how you imagined your character? (See earlier section
  "Character Bios for Dialogue.") If it doesn't, write it again. Write another
  version of it. Or change your character's biography to match what they're
  saying.
- If your characters have a strong purpose and you know what information
  they need to speak, they could say it directly. Or they could say it slanted
  or indirectly. They could also say the opposite, talk around it, *almost* say it
  (reluctantly), or get frustrated trying to say it. This depends on the personal
  agenda of your characters, and whether they are conscious of it or not.
- Have your other characters react appropriately to what another character
  has said or done. "Appropriately" can be surprising depending on their own
  agendas. Have they acknowledged each other in word or gesture?
- Review what you've written. Replace generic words and concepts with specific and colorful ones. Is it entertaining? Could it be more entertaining?
- Read it aloud. How does it sound?
- Every single line of dialogue does not have to be perfect or amazing.

In the following two chapters, there will be various exercises for honing many of
the aforementioned steps. But for now, this is the beginning of dialogue application. You think you know your story enough. You've done your character work
by answering the Character Check Sheet. The character's name is on the page,
and now and you want to begin writing down what she says. You're hesitant. Or
you write something down. You're uncertain about it. Maybe it can be better.
What are you missing?

NG

- Introduction: Better hearing
- Ear tuning
- Nine aspects of dialogue
- Eavesdropping
- Collecting dialogue

Introduction: Better hearing

Among the interesting things about hearing is that you can't not hear. If a car backfires, you'll hear it. You can't block it by stuffing up your ears, because by that point it's too late. You've already heard it. You could be deep in thought and not hear your phone ring from another room. But it's not that you've elected not to hear your phone ring. This is because hearing happens just within your field of consciousness. However, when you focus your attention on the sounds around you, it is suddenly as if you've entered an entirely new universe of sound information that you hadn't realized was always there. But this takes focus. This chapter is about directing your focus on hearing people verbally communicate in greater depth. And in doing so, notice aspects of verbal communication that have always been there, which you just didn't hear, recognize, or consciously process. With practice, you can learn to expand how and what you hear regarding dialogue, and appreciate the music of conversation in all its variations, insights, and subtleties.

Ear tuning

Ear tuning is my term for recalibrating your hearing in order to be able to detect aspects of dialogue that you normally wouldn't. It's like learning a new word and then suddenly coming across it everywhere. That word has always been there but, somehow, you've had a blind spot for it. The term for this phenomenon is *frequency illusion*. It's a cognitive bias that your mind creates. As you learn to hear new aspects of verbal communication, they will initially be fresh in your mind. Then you'll automatically notice them and, with practice, you'll expand your perception to include them in your everyday hearing.

I'm using the concept of "recalibrating" instead of "teaching" or "learning" because, presumably, you can already hear. You don't need to learn to hear. Like understanding and appreciating poetry or music, there's both an intellectual and a visceral, sonic aspect. You can intellectually count the beats and identify the meters within a piece of music, but can you *feel* them or even perceive them on your own? And even if you are guided to listen to a particular range of sounds, can you actually perceive it? This can also be applied to all of the senses. With taste, it's been proven that very few people are even physically capable of detecting the nuances of wine. But with verbal communication, once you fine-tune the focus of your listening attention, you'll be able to hear characteristics of conversations all around you that you can draw from to enhance your own scripted dialogue. This fine-tuning is the recalibration.

By now, if you've made it this far in this book, you are at least familiar with most of the aspects, characteristics, and facets of dialogue that we are recalibrating to hear. We'll go over them now and then move onto specific exercises to enhance your ability to hear and perceive them.

Nine aspects of dialogue

The idea is that going forward, as you perceive verbal communication in life, from screens, or books, you'll be able to hear and identify the following aspects of dialogue and appreciate how they inform the speaker or conversation:

- Sound – Literally the pure sound of words. This includes shiny or irregular sounding words, tics, sonic mannerisms, volume, accents, and alliterations. What do these say about the speaker? Are they erudite, pretentious, musical, lyrical, whimsical, angry, or scattered? It's true that an actor, or any speaker, can add levels of information that might not appear in the written text. But as you hear the pure sounds of what they are speaking, try to visualize how you could describe how they are delivering their lines and sounds on the written page. Would you use ALL CAPS for volume and to express what loudness sounds like; exclamation marks (!) to suggest the sounds of urgency and excitement; or ellipses (…) for the pace, sounds of what's missing, or pausing?
- Tone – Without trying, we immediately pick up on the tone or mood of the speaker. It can be subtle, although it's often easily apparent. What's not apparent is that we, the listener, too often take it for granted rather than mindfully crafting an appropriate response.

- Rhythm – This includes pacing, pauses, tempo, staccato, and line lengths between people talking. Is it a style? Does it reflect anxiousness, nervousness, or tranquility? What. Does. It. Feel. Like. When. Someone. Speaks. This. Rhythm?
- Text and subtext – What is being said directly and what is being said indirectly? How conscious is the speaker of what they are not saying directly, but saying subtextually? Are they avoiding, or just unable to be forthright? Is it out of fear, being inarticulate, or is it entirely unconscious?
- Non sequiturs or nonlinear – These include tangents and abrupt or random changes of subject. How can this express the logic of the character? Does it characterize them as scattered, poetic, or rambling?
- Wants and needs – In real, ordinary conversations, much of what we say is subtext for our wants and needs. When I ask "how ya doin'?", how much of my asking has to do with me really wanting to know, and how much of it has to do with me needing to feel less lonely? How much of what we speak is informed by our wants and needs?
- Content – What is the apparent subject? What is being talked about? Is it interesting, or is it filler? Can easy adjectives and nouns be replaced by more precise and specific words?
- Exposition – Is the content informational and expository, or boring?
- Style – Like many of the aspects listed, we can hear and instantly recognize them without consciously considering them. We automatically perceive if the speaker's personal style is or wants to be perceived as erudite, articulate, cool, streetwise, or hipster-esque, to name but a few. Is the style affected or innate to the speaker?

In real life, we don't parse our conversations into the aforementioned components. When we listen to scripted characters' dialogues, we also don't compartmentalize it. We take it in whole and digest it on the run as we hear it. But when you write dialogue, although you might initially crank it out, you will eventually pay careful attention to many of the aspects listed. Not all of them will be appropriate for every line of dialogue or for every character who speaks. But becoming familiar with these characteristics, to the extent that you can readily hear, identify, and understand their effects, will make your writing and revising all the more purposeful.

Eavesdropping

The following are exercises designed to focus your attention on the various components of verbal communication.

Without being intentionally creepy, if you are going to study conversation, you need to listen, really listen, to as much of it as possible. Overhearing others' speech is the perfect opportunity to focus on what comprises the dynamics of dialogue. Here is a numbered guideline for this exercise:

1. Go to a cafe, pub, mall, or wherever you can listen to others conversing. Or if you are at home, overhear the people you live with. However, the key here is that the people you are overhearing cannot know that you are listening to them.

2. Transcribe two pages of overheard dialogue. Either write it down as you hear it, or record it on your phone and then transcribe it later. Write at least two pages. If you can't find two pages worth of continual dialogue, fill the pages with overheard snippets of dialogue. Ideally, type your overheard dialogue into a scriptwriting program so that you can begin to gauge how much dialogue fills a page. The general rule for film scripts that is one page on the paper equals one minute of screen time. For television, since it's so dialogue-intensive, it is sometimes considered that a bit more than one page equals one minute. Of course, this also includes slug-lines, script direction, and transitions, in addition to the dialogue. But the emphasis is on the dialogue. Keep your script directions minimal and succinct. At first, do not censor what you are overhearing and documenting. Get in the habit of listening to people speaking anywhere, including a single person speaking on the phone, or speaking to him-/herself (like a ranting drunk). Using punctuation as previously discussed, *strive to place the dialogue on the page exactly as it sounds*. This includes not just the words, but also *how* they were spoken. Capitalize a word or sentence if it was said loudly or yelled, and ellipses if sentences trailed off or seemed to pause for an absent word or thought not spoken. Don't forget to write out the "uhs." Or if you hear someone falter or stu-ssttu-stutter a word, literally write it how it sounds, how you heard it.

3. Now you have two pages of authentic, unadulterated verbal communication. This is your petri dish, where you can study and analyze the dialogue with a microscope.

4. As you look over your two pages, consider the following aspects and how, or if, any of them apply: *sound, tone, rhythm, text and subtext, non sequiturs, wants and needs, content, exposition*, and *style*. Can you detect any components of them within your written text?

   (Eventually, avoid absolutely mundane conversations, such as rote interactions.)

5. Repeat 1 to 4 weekly, daily, or as much as you'd like. Focus on a single aspect during a single session. Focus on ones that appeal to you. Become familiar with all of them.

6. Bring the list of dialogue aspects along with you when you are hunting for overheard dialogue. As you listen, glance at your list, and one at a time, simply listen for each aspect separately. For example, just listen for *sounds*. Block out everything else. Then listen for *tone* only. Go through the entire list. Do this repeatedly. Some of the aspects will not apply, and some will. It won't take long before you'll be able to detect many of these aspects simultaneously.

7. Even when you are not consciously documenting overheard conversation, listen to any verbal communication habitually, through the lens of these various dynamics.
8. Apply this perception as you listen or read scripted dialogue from existing film and television.

Here is an example of a student's overheard dialogue at her home. Although she didn't identify in the text who the characters actually were, later she disclosed that they were her brother and father. Can you tell who's who?

```
INT. KITCHEN - EVENING

Sitting at the dining room table, Matt and Larry play
a game of chess - even though neither of them really
know how to play

                    LARRY
          Fine, whatever. That's fine.

                    MATT
          What do you mean that's fine? That's what
          it is.

                    LARRY
          Then, that's what it is.

                    MATT
          It's a stalemate. Whatever move I had,
          see, you fucked that up. You thought, you
          thought, you were doing the right thing.

                    LARRY
          I know that was like a stalemate, I
          didn't know that was the rule.

                    MATT
          Here, you want to replay?

                    LARRY
          Yah, I'll replay. I didn't know that was-

                    MATT
          -It's a stalemate. That's what a stalemate
          is.

                    LARRY
          So, I had to strategically put you in
          checkmate?
```

                    MATT
Yes.

                    LARRY
So, how would I have done that? Like there
is no way I could have done that. Like that
makes no sense.

                    MATT
Yes, it's when you had no moves.

                    LARRY
We both basically had no moves.

                    MATT
No I had moves, but whatever they were,
weren't legal. They were putting myself
in check. Checkmate versus stalemate,
here's the explanation: "Checkmate ends
the game with a clear winner while
stalemate ends in a draw or a tie.
Checkmate requires one player to be in
check and unable to move out of it, while
stalemate requires that the play not be
in check. Both checkmate and stalemate
require one player to not be able to make
a legal move." So, stalemate is I'm not in
check, but wherever I go puts me in check.

                    LARRY
But, I had you basically in checkmate in
both places.

                    MATT
Wherever I went put me in check. But I
wasn't in check already. ... I don't think?

Looking this over, are there any characteristics that stand out? The *sounds* are
fairly ordinary in terms of colorful, charged language, short of "fucked up," and
the repeated sound of "stalemate" and "checkmate." But by repeating "stalemate"
and "checkmate" the *tone* becomes fairly obsessive; there's a nervous aggressive-
ness underpinning the conversation, perhaps repressed anger? The *content* has
to do with the rules of chess, at least *textually*. But *subtextually*, it seems like it's
about winning or being right. Matt *wants* to win, but *needs* to be right, to be
acknowledged for being right. The *expository* explanation about the rules that
Matt reads to Larry informs them both. Larry *wants* to know the rules and *needs*
the harmony that the rules will provide.

Every one of my judgments and interpretations may be entirely untrue for the actual people overheard in the scene. It doesn't matter. Ultimately, these real people are now your imagined creations. We hear things, feel things, and make judgments seamlessly. Get in the habit of noticing how conversations make you feel. Become more conscious of how the content of the conversation affects you and the other participants in the interaction.

Overhearing dialogue, writing it down in proper script format, and then interpreting it through the lens of the nine aspects of dialogue is an invaluable exercise.

Creating characters

Using your overheard dialogue, try filling in the Character Check Sheet (see Chapter 10) for the people who are speaking. Using your imagination based upon what they say, while picturing their physicality (including their expression and attire) and their movements, answer the Character Check Sheet and realize that as you do this, they are becoming your own imagined creations.

Punching up overheard dialogue

Again, using your overheard dialogue, replace dull words with shiny ones and generic nouns with specific ones. Try clipping the last few words or the first few words. Perhaps add an ellipsis or cause a word to be stuttered. Play with making it punchier, more dynamic and entertaining. This is the beginning of *rewriting* or *revising* your dialogue.

Although the overheard dialogue cited earlier was pretty darn good as it was, here's an example of taking the first few passages and playing with them. The changes are in parentheses.

```
                    LARRY
        Fine, whatever. That's fine.

        (Cool. Fine-fine-fine. Whatever!!!)

                    MATT
        What do you mean that's fine? That's what
        it is.

        (Dude, don't lose your shit. That's the
        way it is.)

                    LARRY
        Then, that's what it is.
        (FINE!! That's the fuckin' way it is!)
```

                    MATT
It's a stalemate. Whatever move I had,
see, you fucked that up. You thought, you
thought, you were doing the right thing.

(Dude, it's a stalemate! My bishop's
smithereened by your rook either way.
Ya-ya-you thought you'd pull a Sicilian
Defence, but you d'd'don't have the skills
to pull it--)

                    LARRY
I know that was like a stalemate, I
didn't know that was the rule.

(--Screw you! I wasn't copying a "Sicilian
Defence"!! And I know what a fuckin'
stalemate is "dude"!)

                    MATT
Here, you want to replay?

(K', my bad, dad. We cool? Wanna go again?)

Finding the intention in overheard dialogue

Once again, using your overheard conversation, consider what's *not* being said and write out each character's direct intention as if there were no social filters and they could say exactly what they are thinking or feeling.

Collecting dialogue

When you want to maintain good health, you stick to a basic healthy program: eat nurturing food, get ample sleep, and exercise. There are numerous programs and regimes designed to aid and enhance specific emotional and physical needs that you can institute and try out. But they all include the basics. This is also true with writing generally and writing dialogue specifically, the basics being input, conscious listening, and exercise.

- *Input.* This is being aware of all conversations by anyone within your hearing range. It includes conversations that you are engaged in. It also includes curated dialogue that you elect to listen to and read – films, TV, books, plays, etc.

- *Conscious listening.* Make it a habit of always being attuned to the sounds and rhythms of spoken language. Pay attention to specific words and term usages, and to how others articulate ideas, emotions. What do they say to express or avoid expressing their deeper feelings?
- *Exercise.* This is the act of both writing dialogue for your specific characters and also literally keeping a written record of words, terms, and outstanding snippets of conversation you come across or observe.

Professionals steal

"Amateurs borrow, professionals steal" is a quote attributed to John Lennon, who stole it from T. S. Eliot's quote, "Amateur poets borrow; mature poets steal." No matter who said it, artists of all stripes are constantly borrowing, stealing, and being inspired by each other. Writing dialogue is no different.

Some writers keep a notebook with them all the time and are constantly jotting down their thoughts, insights, scribbles, character traits, and bits of dialogue that they hear or invent. If you are working on a project and have specific characters in mind, it can be particularly helpful to siphon your conscious listening through the mouths of those characters. Try it on for fit. Hear what it sounds like.

Listed in the following is a way to organize, document, and save a wide variety of observed, found, stolen, and created words, sentences, and snippets of dialogue. Aside from keeping you constantly attuned to the sounds of language, you might also be able to use what you have collected on future projects.

Create a folder with three files:

1. File One: Memorable scripted dialogue that you heard or read from films, TV, and plays. This might include famous quotes, passages from speeches, and lines read in blogs and zines.
2. File Two: Random snippets that you overhear. Do not hesitate to grab these gifts.
3. File Three: Invented words, lines, and snippets of dialogue. Once you are in the habit of hearing and saving memorable bits of language, you'll find yourself uttering your own variations, invented words, and original lines.

By routinely adding to the files, you will be actively living in the music of conversations while gathering a treasure chest of language nuggets. The idea is to make conscious listening an integral part of your life and also to make a habit of documenting memorable bits of language that you come across. As you work on various scripted projects, not only will you be able to access these files, but your listening muscles will also stay firm, and you'll be able to more easily enhance your scripted dialogue.

12

VOICE EXERCISES

Introduction: Voice exercises

When we think of a film that is marked with its director's very distinct style, we think primarily about its singular visual style, musical choices, subject matter, and how specifically it makes us feel. When you watch a film by Federico Fellini, it's a distinct Fellini experience. His musical collaborator, Nino Rota, created a specific sound pallet. He mixed melancholic folk melodies with carnivalesque theatrical tonalities that, when combined with Fellini's equally distinct and sometimes bizarre visual imagery, produced a signature experience. This is the same for films by Pedro Almodóvar, Wes Anderson, and Quentin Tarantino. But for the most part, we don't think of these films solely in terms of their dialogue.

True, there are exceptions like Aaron Sorkin, Woody Allen, and Diablo Cody, to name but a few superlative dialogue writers, from whom we've come to expect dialogue with a singular voice. But like Sorkin and Cody, many of the great dialogue writers are primarily screenwriters, not directors, who don't control their projects' casting, music, and visual choices. In fact, many of them are known less for a specific style or voice and more for their high quality of dialogue across a variety of different kinds of stories. Cody's signature work on *Juno* (2007) is not remotely similar to her dialogue in *Young Adult* (2011). But it is still quality, elevated dialogue. Revered screenwriters, like Charlie Kaufman, the Coen Brothers, and even Quentin Tarantino, are also known for their consistently singular content as much as, or more than, their dialogue. Their "voice" is the summation of their unique perception, choices, and attitudes. And although we expect dialogue-heavy scenes from Sorkin, even his brilliantly wordy dialogue isn't always his signature style, as in his screenplays for *Malice* (1993) and *Charlie Wilson's War* (2007). But again, his dialogue is still elevated, smart, and extremely articulate, complete with his nuanced insights that one might even call his Sorkin-isms.

This readily identifiable quality, or voice, is in fact very rare to exist in dialogue alone. We might be able to recognize Woody Allen's pitch-perfect dialogue, but probably only if it emanates from one of his equally recognizably neurotic characters. We could argue that his dialogue creates his characters as much as the other way around, but how would it sound if he were tasked to write a serious film (not a comedy) about an astronaut?

Most screenwriters are very adaptable. They aren't always known for a particular style or absolutely original tonality. It's not that they're voiceless, as much as they have learned how to access the voice of the particular characters they're writing for. Even for screenwriters who bring a specific proclivity toward a certain style of dialogue and content are adept at working their own voice seamlessly into the needs of their characters' voices. How to do this, and then practicing how to do this, is what follows.

Character channeling: Mimicking

There are certain characters we know from a film or TV series who have such strongly defined voices that you only have to recall their names or the title of their film/show to almost immediately hear them in our heads. Carrie Bradshaw from *Sex and the City* (1998), Jules from *Pulp Fiction* (1994), Mark Zuckerberg from *The Social Network* (2010), Larry David from *Curb Your Enthusiasm* (2000), and Elle Woods from *Legally Blonde* (2001) come to mind. If you're not familiar with these examples, watch and listen to them. They are strong, iconic personalities with equally strong and singular voices. If you were hired to be in the writers' room of *Sex and the City*, you'd have to be able to nail Carrie's dialogue in her signature voice – her style, vocal cadence, point of view, and sharply critical yet slightly self-deprecating ruminations on life, love, and fashion.

Like certain hummable songs, certain characters' distinct voices are also nearly hummable. By mimicking them in your mind, you are consciously imitating the sound of their voices, their mannerisms, and the way they carry themselves. In order to do that, you have to think like them, literally. You have to embody them. You have to channel their essences. And it's not that difficult. Once you immerse yourself in their presences and absorb their verbal cadences and attitudes, you'll find that you can also think and speak like them.

Mimicking an existing character can be valuable for improving your own dialogue writing. It's great practice to engage yourself with already formed characters, while also providing you with an alternative voice to channel into your own characters. By doing so, you might find a new hybrid voice that you had not imagined. Or you might simply discover your own character's original voice.

Mimic exercise

1. Identify two existing characters from a film or television show who you want to mimic. Watch the film or the show that they are in, or view a clip of it on YouTube. Ideally, find the screenplay or TV script and read how the characters' lines are written out. Watching and listening, however, is the most important. Certain voices may seem easier or more difficult to inhabit, depending on the specific character you choose. Since you are watching their body languages and expressions as they speak, you might be able to imitate them very quickly.
2. Mimicking the voice of your two chosen characters, write two separate scenes that have the exact same parameters: In each scene, the characters who you are mimicking desperately want something, but encounter opposition. You need to invent what it is that they want. You are free to create any situation around this, including other characters.

The point of this exercise is to see that by channeling different voices, it will automatically dictate different sets of actions, even within the same scene. In the upcoming first example, a student has channeled Mark Zuckerberg from *The Social Network*. Anyone who has seen this film knows that Mark is portrayed very specifically – brilliant; myopically focused; arrogant; condescendingly tone-deaf; and speaks in a quick, deliberate, and nearly robotic cadence.

In the second scene, the same student channels Carrie Mathison from the series *Homeland* (2011). Carrie has a high strung, hyper-personality. She is more action-oriented than verbal, extremely intelligent, manically driven, and wrestles with a bipolar disorder.

The invented parameter of both of the following scenes is that the character is in a cafeteria and needs to deal with push back for wanting additional guacamole. Read and listen:

```
INT. COLLEGE CANTEEN - NIGHT

MARK ZUCKERBERG, 19, taps his student ID repeatedly
and anxiously against the serving counter. He's
wearing his most robust all-nighter outfit--a navy
hoodie and gray jogging pants that perfectly hide any
spots and stains left on them. Two STUDENTS, tired and
impatient, wait in line behind Mark a few steps away.

HANNAH, 52, the serving lady, ready to go home after
a long shift but still keeps up a professional look,
emerges from the back kitchen with a freshly made
```

burrito bowl, closes a plastic lid on it and puts it
down on top of the counter. Mark doesn't take it.

                    MARK
Excuse me, where's my extra guacamole?

Hannah tilts the container to Mark so that he sees the
guac
topping on his food.

                  MARK (CONT'D)
         No, I ordered extra guacamole in a
         separate container.

He's not mad, but rather just stating a fact. For the
first time, Hannah eyes Mark for real. She presses
her lips.

                   HANNAH
         I told you I can't do that.

                    MARK
         I'll pay separately with my credit
         card.

                   HANNAH
         We only do set meals.

                    MARK
         I don't understand where the problem
         is. It's the same amount of food but
         only with divided placement. If I
         wanted guacamole on top of my rice, I
         would just tell you directly.

                   HANNAH
         I can't charge you that way in the -

                    MARK
         Charge it as a second meal, then.

                   HANNAH
         I don't have the power to make that
         decision.

Students behind Mark start to fidget and make small
noises.
Mark doesn't seem to notice.

                    MARK
        You don't need to make that decision.
        I'm making it for you because I'm the
        person paying for it.

                    HANNAH
        Yeah, but you don't pay me to work
        late-night here. My company does. So
        you either take your food and swipe
        for it, or you can file with my
        manager tomorrow just because you
        wanted me to break the guidelines,
        young man.

Stalemate. Hannah looks into Mark's eyes tiredly while
Mark
looks off into a distance.

                    STUDENT #1
        Just take it. Food get mixed up in
        your stomach anyways.

Mark concedes. He grabs his bowl, swipes his ID at the
check-out. He stops by student #1's side.

                    MARK
        That's false, because even though your
        stomach lets all the food enter, only
        proteins get digested in there, so
        food particles would still remain
        separate.
Student #1 stares at Mark as if he's ridiculous.

                    STUDENT #2
        Go to Chipotle.

                    MARK
        I thought they are Chipotle.

EDUARDO, Mark's best friend rushes in.

                    EDUARDO
        What took you so long?

                    MARK
        Bureaucratic capitalism failed me.

Anyone who has seen *The Social Network* will readily recognize this version of Mark Zuckerberg as envisioned by the screenwriter Aaron Sorkin. By mimicking Mark's persona, the student who wrote this was able to project Sorkin's version into her own creation. When Mark says, "I don't understand where the problem is. It's the same amount of food but only with divided placement," he's using uncommon terminology unnecessarily. He expresses his arrogance by showing off his "intelligence" and then does it again as he corrects another student by saying, "That's false, because even though your stomach lets all the food enter, only proteins get digested in there, so food particles would still remain separate." Ultimately, he doesn't succeed in his quest for more guacamole. This is possibly because he has misread how to handle the situation, including not realizing which restaurant he is in, and quickly made Hannah an adversary. At the end, he rationalizes his own shortcoming with, "Bureaucratic capitalism failed me."

In this second version of this scene, an entirely different set of actions occur through mimicking another character.

```
INT. HEADQUARTERS CANTEEN - DAY
Lunch time almost ends. CARRIE MATHISON rushes in in
her
usual office attire and a clipboard in hand. HANNAH,
52, is emptying up table pans from behind the serving
counter.
Carrie greets Hannah, a little out of breath.


                    CARRIE
          Hannah!


                    HANNAH
          Wow, slow down, Carrie.



Hannah wipes down spills on the countertop.


                 HANNAH (CONT'D)
          It's good to see you. But we're
          closing. Only stuff in the fridge are
          available now.

Carrie, clearly disappointed at her words, decides to
persist.


                    CARRIE
          Listen, can you please please do me a
          favor and see if you have any
```

guacamole left in the kitchen? I'll
buy them all. This is work-related and
time-sensitive.

Hannah is confused.

>   HANNAH
>   Okay? I'll take a look but guac
>   usually goes out really fast. Hold on.

Hannah disappears behind the kitchen door and re-
emerges with a serving container with brown guac
remainders at the very bottom. She scrapes some off
with a clean spoon.

>   HANNAH (CONT'D)
>   This isn't edible, Sweetie. I can't
>   sell this to you.

Carrie beams with pleasure at the sight of it.

>   CARRIE
>   No-no-no, this would suffice. I'll take it!

Hannah studies her with doubt, making Carrie aware
that she hasn't explained things properly.

>   CARRIE (CONT'D)
>   I'm not gonna eat it. It's for
>   experimenting.

>   HANNAH
>   Well, you do your thing, but I can't
>   sell you stale food. It'll get me
>   fired.

Hannah drops the stuff on the counter, crossing her
arms. Carrie eyes the serving container in distress.

>   HANNAH
>   (softer)
>   ...If you really need guac, call
>   delivery.

                          CARRIE
            That takes too much time. I have an
            entire room of people waiting for me
            upstairs.

Hannah wonders, but she knows better than asking. She
looks
around.

                          HANNAH
            Well, there are guacamole sandwiches
            in the fridge over there, if that
            helps.

Carrie is so happy she reaches out over the counter to
hug
Hannah.

                          CARRIE
            Oh my goodness, Hannah, you just saved
            my day. Thank you so much.

Carrie runs to grab seven sandwiches for check out.
She grabs a spoon from the utensil box, sits at an
empty table, tears open a sandwich, scrapes off the
guacamole and piles it up on the wrapping paper.

With a different personality, even though it's the same basic setup, we get an entirely different situation and set of responses. Here we see Carrie's unwillingness to take no for an answer, while being nimble enough to work with what she has. When she answers, "No-no-no, this would suffice. I'll take it!" we get a sense of her manic enthusiasm. And when she finds and executes a solution at the end, it's less about what she says and more about what she does.

Practicing this mimic exercise on a simple scene can help you hone your ability and confidence in imitation. Trying out an existing character's voice on your own characters, and in your own scripts, can lead you to discover new events and responses that you wouldn't imagine otherwise. By mimicking, you're accessing not only an entirely new voice, but also an entire personality and set of actions that come along with it.

Character channeling: Other voices

If you can imagine channeling a preexisting character's voice in order to explore possibilities for your own characters, don't stop there. Focusing on other types of characters might additionally expand your options while giving you unique ways in which your characters could speak.

Generic voice exercise

1. Use the same scene parameter that we used before: Your main character desperately wants something, but encounters opposition. You need to invent what it is that they want. You are free to create any situation around this, including other characters.
2. This time, instead of a known, completely formed character, write your scene imagining your character as a sweet child; a mean child; a mathematician; a criminal; a plumber. Add to this list any other generic characters that you want. You can add generic archetypes that you want to explore or try out because they match something that you are working on. Don't be limited in your experimentation.

Monologue exercise

1. Go to your favorite people-watching locale and pick a person who commands your interest. If no one seems to stick out for you, then choose someone randomly. Although overhearing them is fine, it's more important to observe their movements, actions or inactions, physicality, body language, choice of clothing, hair styling, etc.
2. Focusing on them, pretend that you are hearing their voice-over in a movie as they narrate about themselves to the audience. Be open to listening to the torrent of uncontrolled thoughts and judgments you might be making. While imagining their voice-over, consider using both your positive and negative judgments. The moment that you write your thoughts in a first-person voice, things can change. You might make a snap judgement and think "he's a dirty slob." But the moment that you change it to "I'm a dirty slob" or "I know that everyone thinks I'm a dirty slob," it begins to mean something else. Is the person being deliberately self-denigrating and honestly self-aware? Is he sarcastic, cynical, or just clinically truthful? Obviously, if you do this, then you must start with yourself and your own thoughts.
3. Write a one-page voice-over monologue that reveals the person's longings, aspirations, and deepest or darkest secrets.
4. Do it again for another random person you observe. Then do it again.

As you write this out, remember that it might be very difficult for the people to say the words that you are making them say. Or, since the words now belong to the characters and not you, make it extremely difficult for them to verbally express their most intimate thoughts. Given that it is painfully difficult, they might have many pauses. They might falter or stutter a line that they are hesitant to say aloud. They might start and stop, and start over while in mid-sentence. Write out their dialogue precisely as you envision it being spoken.

Subtext exercise

1. Reimagine two characters, who you have already written monologues for, as romantic partners. Write a conversation between them in which one person wants to tell the other that they want to break up, but they can never say it directly.
2. This time, write a conversation in which you imagine that one of them wants to tell the other that they love them, but they just can't say "I love you" no matter how hard the person tries.

The idea here is to create dialogue that focuses on what is not being said, or what cannot be said, in order to access the subtext. Sometimes people will consciously or unconsciously be unable to state their feelings out of fear, embarrassment, or simply an inability to express their feelings. When people do this, they speak subtextually and never say it directly. Practice writing around direct feelings, wants, or needs. Using metaphors, symbols, and images instead of direct communication is one of the ways that people speak subtextually. For example, someone might say, "We're like two tennis players stuck at match point." Other people tell stories or talk about another person when they're actually speaking about themselves. One could say, "I know someone who loved their cat so much that he was willing to mortgage his home to pay the vet bill."

Hearing and improving your own voice

As much as we try, it's impossible not to be ourselves. Even our various attempts to embrace other personas and beliefs are still us. And it is common among artists and writers to be obsessed with finding and articulating their own uniquely singular imprint on the world. We are envious of those who seem to effortlessly create work that is none other than theirs alone. For some of them, it is in fact effortless and they can't help but create everything in a particularly distinct fashion. For others, what we consider a signature voice actually developed after years of toiling in other directions. Some successful screen and television writers have written primarily in the same tonality most of their careers. They are known for and are branded as "science fiction writers," "romantic comedy writers," etc. Others have had successful careers writing in all kinds of different genres. There are no rules.

Sometimes screenwriters, and especially new ones, don't trust their instincts. This is particularly true when writing dialogue. They don't like that what they've come up with seems too random. They want their ideas and dialogue to be less arbitrary and more consistent with their own vision of things. They want some assurance that what they create is theirs alone, and emanates from their personal uniqueness. As valid as all of these considerations are, one forgets that the unifying factor in all the random arbitrariness is still you, the person who came up with these ideas. It's true that not every idea or the first thing that pops into your mind is necessarily a keeper. But it might be.

For those struggling to distinguish their own personal style but can't, I ask this question: Are you willing to only write in a single style for the rest of your life? Again, some writers are perfectly happy writing dialogue for action movies until the day that they die. For others, being locked into an expected style is a curse. But for those who struggle with the notion of articulating their personal voice, let me offer this suggestion: In the first draft, write it the way that you hear it. If you are inside your character, write it the way that your character says it. If you are mimicking another character, write it the way in which you envision that character would say it. Whatever you write, it all comes from you. And that's just the beginning.

Maybe you wrote some killer dialogue right off the bat. You did it. There's no need to change a word. Maybe it's just sitting there taking up space, and you know in your bones that it could be better. This entire book has been about the various aspects and nuances of dialogue and the tools to rework it. The notion of improvement is also subjective. You can strive to improve something, yet find that you've made it worse. But it's easy to change that. Delete it. Try again.

Identify the kind of dialogue that you really love hearing. Aspire to write like that. Do the exercises that have been offered in this book through the lens of styles that you like the most. Immerse yourself in the kinds of dialogue that you want to write. Listen to it. Read it. Live with it. On your first pass, if you are not inspired, then write it straight and keep it simple. Strive for clarity. On your next pass, consider what it is that you're trying to do. How would you like it to sound? Imagine the ideal movie star for the part saying the words. Write it for them. Tailor it for them. How does it sound? Is it sounding too much like another known character, or is it too obvious? Then rethink it. Approach it from another angle. Apply what you've gleaned in this book. Find better, more interesting, and specific words or idioms. Consider how your character speaks their lines. Replicating how they sound in the written word might alone give it the uniqueness or originality that you seek.

The following is an example that may or may not be to everyone's liking. It's from the Amazon Prime series *Hunters* (2020). It's clear that in this series, the writers were tasked to push much of their dialogue in as unique a fashion as they could. Simple things are said in wonderfully convoluted and creatively colorful ways. The following dialogue appears after the Nazi "hunters" have found a person, The Ghost, murdered and unrecognizably disfigured. Sister Harriet reveals to them what she discovered that the Nazis have been up to:

> Sister Harriet
> ...No Kristellnacht, no cattle cars, no camps,
> no crematoria, now just a series of
> manufactured cells.

She's referring to biological cells as in bioterrorism. One of the team members, Lonny Flash, connects the dots and realizes that this information now answers why the victim, The Ghost, was so disfigured. There are a million ways Lonny Flash or anyone could verbalize this realization. How about: "Ah, so that's why The Ghost was so disfigured!" or "Damn, if that's what happened to The Ghost, god help the rest of us," and so on and on. And let's say you wrote it like I just did. Unless either someone else told you to beef it up or you told yourself that, there might not be any reason to mess with it. Of course, I have not yet mentioned that the character of Lonny Flash is the type of person who likes to speak in hyperbole and self-congratulatory exclamations. So maybe this dialogue could be punchier. This is what Lonny Flash actually says in the series:

> Lonny Flash
> So, that's what made The Ghost look like
> what Zsa Zsa Gabor leaves in the toilet
> after borscht night at Milos Forman's...?

As I said, this might not be for everyone. You might think it's great or you might think, "What the hell is he talking about?" It doesn't matter. What matters is that, like it or not, it's colorful and, at least for those who enjoy this series, it's entertaining. I should insert here that those who produce and fund this series also consider this entertaining. If you were tasked to write a certain character's dialogue in such a way that whenever they spoke they talked like Lonny Flash, full of hyperbole and crazy pop references, you could. It wouldn't be exactly the same if you wrote it. Your crazy references and nearly arbitrary thought choices would be yours alone. But you could do it once you had a sense of what the task is and who your character is. You could also *invent* a character who speaks as wildly as this. You would simply need to sit down and understand who he is. The point is, it's all possible and it all comes from you. Remember, dialogue expresses the way that the character's mind works. You're the facilitator.

Improvisation

In many ways, at least for first drafts in which you are more or less dictating what you imagine your characters are saying, the entire process is improvisational. We can never know our next thought until we think it ... or write it.

The notion of improvisation, or "improv," has always been a mainstay in the arsenal of acting techniques and exercises. It can certainly help actors be nimbler, in the moment, and creative. It can also help an actor's confidence. Being on stage before a live audience is akin to high-wire tightrope walking without a net. Therefore, being able to salvage a flubbed or dropped line is essential. Being prepared and able to do that goes a long way toward having the guts and swagger to stand on the stage at all.

Writers, on the other hand, have purposely elected not to put themselves in front of others and do not have to perform on the spot. We like to write in the privacy of our own safe and secure spaces, far from the pressure of having to "save" the moment from crashing down. We like to be able to write, rewrite, and revise before we show it to anyone. Writers definitely have their own set of neurosis and issues to deal with, but live audiences are usually not among them. However, working in a television writers' room in which you are being paid handsomely to contribute great ideas, often in the presence of other writers and producers, can definitely be stressful. When we consider improv for screenwriters, it's less about learning to be prepared for the unexpected, and more about freeing up the possibilities of dialogue, freeing up the creative juices, and exploring the unexplored.

Larry David, the cocreator of *Seinfeld* (1989) and the creator of *Curb Your Enthusiasm* (2000), said about *Curb*, "I don't write shows with dialogue where actors have to memorize dialogue. I write the scenes where we know everything that's going to happen. There's an outline of about seven or eight pages, and then we improvise it." Here we have a perfect blend of great improv actors and terrific writers. However, most screen and television writers aspire to write a great script with great dialogue, not a finished, produced show based on their outlines.

Examining basic improv acting techniques is a good place to start to find ways in which we can use them for writing or enhancing our written dialogue. Not unlike a writer, the actor who must spontaneously improvise based on a word, concept, or situation needs to, on some level, embody that word or concept in order to react to and act like it. Similarly, as a writer, no matter what the character or subject matter is and no matter what emerges spontaneously, it originates singularly from inside yourself. Improvising is always an individual, intuitive activity. Even if there are numerous improvers, each person improvs uniquely.

"Say 'yes, and ...'" for actors

Remember the purpose of improv is to be able to spontaneously take something, anything, a word, concept, idea, information, or character trait, and run with it. "Run" implies going forward and keeping it moving. And as actors perform their improvisation in front of others, it is equally important to keep it entertaining and compelling. But more than anything else, the initial objective between improv actors is to keep their scene alive. That is why the first and primary cardinal rule of improv for actors is "Say 'yes, and...'" It's the mode of reacting to each other.

Since the purpose is to propel the scene forward, the idea of "say 'yes'" is to not inhibit or deny the moment, but to agree with it. You encourage your improv partner… "and…" then add an entertaining statement, concept, or information building on or reacting to what was just said. Then the other actor reacts yet again by "saying 'yes … and …'" by agreeing and then making another entertaining statement, back and forth and so on. By following the last line of the other, a narrative emerges. A line of building blocks begins to take shape. How creative or compelling the actors are will determine how successful the story is. Also, one of the important rules of improv is "there are no mistakes." If one actor fumbles the ball, the next actor picks it, and hurtles it forward. On stage, you're desperately trying to avoid "dead air." You are either able to continue the conversation/story or not. And allowing for mistakes, or actually considering them potential assets, is not only liberating, but also a good work ethic.

"Say 'no, but…'" for writers

When you write dialogue, especially the first draft, you too are spontaneously pulling words out of the air. But not entirely. You may not know the precise words before you write them down, but you often know what the objective of the scene is, and hopefully what the goals, wants, and needs of the character as well. But since, as previously discussed in depth, strong dialogue is steeped in variations of conflict, the dialogue writer might be better served with reacting with "Say 'no, but…'" than with compulsive acceptance. This way, rather than automatically acquiescing and upholding the previous statement made, consider reacting by denying it and finding a "but" in order to find a conflict to keep the story moving.

Denying is a form of conflict. And it has infinite shades. By denying, I'm not emphatically saying that you should consider every reaction to be a hard "no!" Although "no" or an abject abnegation as a form of reacting to what was previously said should not be completely ruled out. In an office setting, for example, a simple request of "can I borrow your pen?" can be answered with a "no," which can lead to revealing all sorts of more interesting character traits. "No, you cannot borrow my pen because the last time you 'borrowed' my stapler you never gave it back!" says something about both characters' personalities. Or, "No. Only if you get me tickets to the Mets game," shows how a fun flirtation or office politics can also be entwined into the fabric of the story.

"No," or denying a statement as a reaction might come in the guise of denigration, sarcasm, or any other less-than-positive attitudes. It's not outright denying, but rather placing a negative judgment as a reaction. Denigrating is also full of conflict. So is being snarky, abrasive, judgmental, offensive, and gamy. Reactions with these attitudes are more in the "No" category than in the "Yes" category and might lead your dialogue in a more energetic and compelling direction. To be clear, you don't have to always rule out a positive or "Say yes, and …" response. But for dialogue definitely consider "Say no, but …" as your default.

Beyond "Say no, but…" as a reaction to each other's lines, consider another improv technique to enhance your dialogue. In acting improv, it is common for the improv performers to solicit from the audience a specific word or noun, like a name of a vegetable. And then once, let's say "asparagus," is accepted, then the actors begin to spontaneously improvise a story around asparagus. For screenwriters, it's much more situational. You arrive at a scene that you are about to write. You likely already know what information you'll need to convey in this scene. Some of that information will be conveyed visually, meaning we'll actually see your character do something that unto itself conveys a lot. Some instructors might suggest that you don't really need to say anything more if it can be conveyed visually. But I believe that to be a far too reductionist conclusion, and that many of the films and television shows that we love are strewn with characters' dialogue alongside and/or even despite their actions. In *Pulp Fiction*, when Jules and Vincent drive to their target's apartment, enter, assassinate most everyone there, and reclaim a coveted briefcase, it is their dialogue, especially Jules's, that we remember. It's also Jules's dialogue that makes the scene so incredibly and amusingly tense.

How do you know when to add dialogue or not? Since you're reading this book on writing dialogue, let's assume that you too enjoy great entertaining dialogue whenever possible. Let's imagine you want to improv the *Pulp Fiction* scene that was just described. You know that your two characters are hitmen. You know that they are tasked with retrieving a briefcase and punishing those who have it. So now you have your basic parameters of the scene. Now you need to investigate the character traits of your two hitmen. One of them, Vincent, is laconic and not as verbose as Jules. Jules is a talker. Now you can start your improvising. With another person, a creative friend or a writer, have each person play the part of either Jules or Vincent. Start the scene: They knock on the door and...? Play it out. Remember "Say no, but..." One of the inhabitants says, "Who's there?" and your Jules actor says, "Jules and Vincent, let us in!" Maybe the inhabitant says, "No, but come back tomorrow. I have the measles and it's very contagious." Maybe Vincent says to Jules, "My immune system is fairly compromised and I can't afford to miss any more days of work, so let's come back tomorrow." Then perhaps Jules says, "Sure, no problem," as he draws from his coat an Uzi and pellets the door open with bullets. Jules might respond with, "Wouldn't want you to get the fuckin' flu." And maybe Vincent answers, "The flu would be fine, it's the measles I'm afraid of," as he lifts his coat lapel over his mouth and nose and in slow motion slides his .357 Magnum from his shoulder holster and fires three rounds into face of the first inhabitant standing in the blown-open doorway. And on and on. How would you imagine it? What if you gave Vincent a lisp as he quotes the first law of thermodynamics while nonchalantly blasting away. How would that play?

Dialogue improvisation

1. Keep "Say no, but..." as your default. Make conflict and obstacles your friend.

2. Have your improv partners ready. Each person assumes a character in the scene. If you are alone, literally stand up and assume each character from different positions.

3. Define the basic parameter of the scene and convey it to your improv partner(s). What is its purpose? What information do you want to convey that is essential to understand the story? Write a list of information that you might want to convey on a board so that everyone can see it during the improv.

4. What traits do you envision for the characters involved? Or what information do you want to convey about the characters? Convey this to your improv partners. Include physical attributes or disabilities. If you're not sure or don't know, be open to discovering it during the improv.

5. Define the physicality and real estate of the scene. Agree where everything physically is in the space that you're working in.

6. Agree on how and where you're starting.

7. The first person starts and the others react. "Say no, but ..." However, be open to "Say yes, and ..." Physically act out, or pantomime, any action that emerges.

8. Play the scene out.

9. Do it again. Change the character that you each play. Do it again.

10. Consider changing the perimeter of the scene.

11. From what you've learned through the improv, play it again with specifics. For example, if one of you improvised a character having a limp or asthma, and you want to further explore that possibility, play the scene again with that specific character trait in mind.

12. Take notes of anything memorable. Maybe even record the entire improv.

13. Use whatever you can for dialogue in your script.

14. Do this entire list or pick and choose.

Obviously, the quality of what you come up with depends on the quality and creativity of the participants. But as an icebreaker, especially if you're stuck, any improvisation can be helpful.

For many writers, a version of this entire process occurs in their minds as they sit alone, hovering over their keyboards. Pausing their flow, or wherever they're at in the story, in order to find improv partners, then setting up a time and place to meet is a huge ordeal that they'd never consider. But you can do it if you want to. It's about spurring creativity and potential, whatever it may take.

FADE OUT: CONCLUSION

Throughout this book, I've repeatedly used music as a metaphor for dialogue. In my mind's ear, I've imagined great dialogue as an equivalent to the inspired riffs by musicians of the great horn, guitar, and piano, whom I love. I get how intimidating that might seem for people who are insecure about their ability to write fine dialogue. But remember, those riffing musicians are usually only a single component in a band of other musicians, all playing the same composed music that has been rigorously rehearsed. Of course, *dialogue* is a major component in the constellation of a completed screenplay. But it is indelibly charged and informed by the script's various components, including each character within every situation of every scene, that when connected, form a compelling narrative journey. And although we've focused on the dialogue in film and television, we can spend another book-length amount of time on writing the script directions – those essential descriptions that set the stage, describe images as they tonally contextualize the dialogue, and conjure a complete film or TV experience for the reader. And finally, we can spend a tome's length of time on the subject of story and script structure.

So let's put dialogue in perspective. It's huge, important, and essential, but it is not freestanding. An amazing situation will more easily inspire appropriate dialogue than one with less purpose. I did say *appropriate* dialogue. I did not say great, inspired, or absolutely memorable. Because even without spectacular dialogue, if the events of a scene itself are creative and inspired, then that scene will be compelling and memorable. Similarly, if a character is so uniquely defined by her actions, then that alone can do much of the heavy lifting. Switching metaphors, great dialogue is the cherry on top; it's the yummy frosting on an otherwise basic cake. Or it's on a fabulous cake. Or it's an entirely spectacular frosted cake!

For those of us who love language, and especially spoken language, great dialogue in film and television can tickle our minds and hearts. We are all musicians of dialogue. We all come with our instruments of voice. It is my hope that this book has helped to lessen your fears, and given you ideas to ponder, tools to use, and methods to practice. And along the way, I hope it has given you a greater understanding of the depth and joys of fine dialogue and the inspiration to write it.

INDEX